Bumper Book of Storytelling into Writing – Key Stage 2

Bumper Book of Storytelling into Writing – Key Stage 2

Pie Corbett

Clown Publishing

First published in 2007 by
Clown Publishing
7 Ferris Grove, Melksham, SN12 7 JW

Copyright © Pie Corbett 2007

A catalogue record for this book is available from the
British Library

ISBN-10 0-9553008-1-9
ISBN-13 978-09553008-1-3

Cover design by Peter Hardy
Clown by
The Mead School, Trowbridge, Wiltshire
Typesetting and Design by Dorwyn, Wells, Somerset
Printed by Butler Tanner and Dennis Ltd, Frome, Somerset

Contents

Introduction

'How did Bob Dylan learn? By learning traditional songs. Creativity is about recreating. Learn other people's songs, then innovate.'

Patrick Lynch, in the Times, 6/3/07.

What is this book?

This book is a resource bank for teachers in key stage 2 who are beginning to develop storymaking as part of their curriculum. Ideally, the process of storymaking will have already been established in key stage 1 and the children will arrive in year three having already built up a bank of well-known tales. However, you may be starting storymaking for the first time. If so, take a look at the section on page xx titled 'First Timers'.

In the book, I have outlined the underlying principles of storymaking and a range of teaching strategies as well as including a bank of stories for teachers to use. Whilst this may well be handy in saving time, I hope that teachers will develop other stories with their different classes and add these to their repertoire. I have suggested a number of useful source books in the appendices. In this book I have focussed upon using traditional tales as a spine for children's own retelling. But we should also remember that children need to tell stories based directly on their own lives because ultimately they will draw upon their own experience as well as their experience of literary stories to create their own tales.

The process of storymaking is a set of understandings that teachers have been developing over the last eight years. It is not a rigid set of rules – and needs to be approached creatively and thoughtfully, adapting as new insights are gained.

Narrative is a primary act of mind

Storytelling is a natural human activity. The expectation that everyone should be able to write is only really a recent idea. The more we have worked on narrative, the more I have become aware that narrative is an essential way of thinking but also that humans are storymaking machines- it is a constant, natural thread through our lives. Starting with oral stories means that we are tapping into a natural process. Writing is tough – especially for many small children! But telling stories is a natural human activity. The brain is constantly retelling the tale of what has happened to us or thinking forwards about what might happen. Our minds buzz with stories of our lives – gossip and anecdotes as well as the basic patterning of everyday life.

Why storymaking?

About eight years ago almost every school I visited was struggling to raise standards in writing. Sometimes the children's writing was lagging way behind their reading ... and I began to wonder why this might be so. What I had noticed was that the best writers were

Introduction

always children who read avidly. It seemed obvious that these children had to be internalising narrative patterns – the language of stories – and then recycling them in their writing.

I knew that toddlers who were read to at home did this because I had noticed my own children recycling phrases from their reading. I began sharing this thought with teachers. It soon became obvious that there was a phase that all children who are read to regularly at home pass through. They alight upon a favourite story that they like to have read again and again (usually something thrilling like 'Topsy and Tim go shopping'). What is intriguing about this is that the children inevitably learn the whole story, word for word, through constant, repetitive re-reading.

These children will then reuse some of the language that they have internalised – they start playing with the language. I remember Poppy, when she was only about two and a half, hearing a knock on the door and saying, "Daddy, it's a little bit early for customers!" That was a direct quote from Granny Goggins – we were in the Postman Pat phase! I noticed too that it was easy enough to make stories up with Poppy – because she had a bank of structures, characters, settings and possibilities to draw upon and reuse.

This thinking lead onto the simple realisation that in order to write any text type, the writer has to be very familiar with it – and this comes most powerfully through repetitive re-reading or being read to. Of course, small children do not read – they hear the language being read to them and often join in, saying the words aloud. This lead me onto the idea that a powerful way to internalise language patterns comes through 'hearing it' and 'saying it' – talking the text type.

Of course, if you want to write a text type it may well be that seeing it written down will also be of use. However, at this point the literacy strategy in England was emphasising the move from reading into writing – but not yet building in the importance of 'talking the text type'. I was meeting many teachers who felt that the reason that the writing was poor was because the children were unimaginative or watched too much TV! I was fast coming to the conclusion that what we needed to do was find strategies to help children internalise patterns of language that could then be called upon to help them compose. In other words, the issue was not so much a lack of the ability to imagine – but rather a lack of the building blocks with which to be imaginative.

I noticed that when teachers were teaching, they started with a model text and then moved into writing. The difficulty seemed to be that they did not loiter with the model for long enough – so that when the children came to write you could not see the underlying patterns reflected in their writing.

The storymaking process begins with this idea of 'loitering' with the model text – finding strategies to make it memorable so that the text enters the child's long-term working memory – only moving on when the children really know the model well.... so well, that they have embedded the text in their minds – irrevocably and forever. Language is learned by:

Introduction

- Repetition – the patterns we want the children to internalise and embed into their linguistic competence have to be repeated;
- Memorable – the patterns they retail and reuse are memorable for some reason – they sound funny, get a job done, label the world;
- Meaningful – the patterns need to be meaningful so that the children can recycle the underlying grammatical structure and therefore generate endless versions of a sentence pattern.

The Story Storehouse – Blueprints for the Imagination

The idea of building a storehouse of stories inside the mind lies at the heart of storymaking. What would happen if in 'foundation stage' children learned about ten simple stories – and then added in another ten in year 1? They would enter year two with about twenty stories to draw upon when writing. Thereafter, we might learn about one every half term – giving the children a bank of about 50 stories by the time they left the primary school. The story storehouse would provide a bank of ideas and patterns to draw upon in their own writing. The idea of 'internalising language patterns' lies at different levels:

1. First of all there is the underlying narrative pattern – the big shape of the story – the story 'pathway'. Rather like internalising a writing frame. Over the last few years, it has become increasingly obvious that there are only a few underlying patterns that are constantly recycled.
2. Secondly, children internalise the major building blocks of narrative – character, setting, action, suspense, dilemma, resolution, opening and ending.
3. Next, children internalise the flow of the sentences. The way in which sentences in stories are not the same as sentences in speech. For instance, a sentence might start with a preposition (*'across the road was an old house'; 'in a distant valley lived a giant'*).
4. Finally, children internalise vocabulary – building up their store of language. In particular, gathering a broader bank of connectives with which to link and structure narrative patterns.

The point about hearing and telling stories is that this is the most powerful way of acquiring language – speaking and listening is how children learn language. The storymaking process aims to help children embed into their daily linguistic competence the structures that are needed for them to create narratives ultimately for themselves.

Whilst I was visiting schools, I began asking reception children if they knew any stories and very soon discovered that many children knew no stories – or if they did know some, they could not retell any as whole tales. Occasionally I would meet a child who would launch into a tale full of gusto and verve – and it was obvious that somebody had read to them or told them stories. I could hear the rhythm of the adult's telling coming through the child's voice.

Introduction

Research I carried out at the 'International Learning and Research Centre' supported this, showing that on entry to school only 2% of children could retell a whole story. I am indebted to Mary Rose and the many teachers whom we worked with at the centre on the original research projects into Storymaking – which were funded by the DFES Innovations unit. The teachers contributed so generously, opening their classrooms and minds as we developed our thinking. I am grateful to all those who continue to contribute their thinking – especially to Mary for her wisdom, her enquiring mind and her focus upon setting up situations within which we could learn together. I have gathered further insights from groups across the country including teachers on the Isle of Wight, in Bradford, Denbighshire and elsewhere – all whom have helped me shape my thinking as we have travel on this story journey.

The impact of the storymaking project is reflected in the new literacy framework, which now has a storytelling strand in every primary year. Though the importance of storytelling had already been recognised in the 'Writing Narrative' flier that the National Literacy Strategy sent to every primary school back in 2001. (The flier came from some writing that I had done with the author David Almond (who wrote 'Skellig') for the key stage 3 strategy). We began by stating that *'story writing is magical – its appeal lies in the creation of imaginative worlds. Stories help us to enthral, to intrigue, to entertain, to wonder and to bring our world and ourselves alive. There is a strong cycle that links reading, discussing, telling, listening and writing.... The roots of story writing lie in a rich experience of listening to and watching stories, drama and role play, early story reading, frequent re-reading of favourites and the telling/retelling of all forms of story'.* We then went on to introduce the following 'principle' that underpins narrative writing (and that this book explores in detail):

- ■ **Imitation** – *early story composition can be based on well-loved tales.*

- ■ **Innovation** – *encourage young writers to base their stories on known tales, making changes to characters, settings or events.*

- ■ **Invention** – *as young writers acquire a good store of stories, they can mix the ingredients and invent their own.'*

This book describes the process of building up the bank of stories. The approach is multi-sensory, primarily oral – learning stories by heart so that the children can retell them or call upon them to fashion new tales of their own. When telling the stories, children use actions and a story map as a visual reminder. There are of course other strategies to help children internalise language that need to run alongside storymaking – a rich vein of story reading, poetry, drama and use of film and visual literacy plus interactive talk are all essential.

The 3 'Eyes'

A storymaking classroom or school has at its heart three approaches which are constantly employed. Many schools have decided that storymaking is something that happens daily. This is useful in areas where children arrive in school not having been read to at home and

Introduction

where children have English as a new language. Story is the bridge from communication and language into literacy.

1. **Imitation** – this is the ability to learning to retell a story so that the child has a bank of tales by heart. Indeed, the stories are known so well that they have become part of the long-term working memory, embedded into their linguistic competence.
2. **Innovation** – this is the ability to adapt a well-known story, in order to create a new story. This may be by making simple changes or a complex retelling. In many schools imitation and innovation is a daily activity – the children are either learning to retell the story or moving on to embellishing or changing it.
3. **Invention** – this is the ability to draw upon the full range of stories, and one's life, to create something new. There may well be elements from different tales as well as totally new ideas. In many schools invention happens once a week or is saved till the class are working on a story unit.

Finally

'Reading is the creative centre of a writer's life', Stephen King.

Over the last five years there has been an increasing interest in storymaking as an effective process that helps children build up their bank of stories and move into creating their own. Many schools across the country and abroad have been using the approach and discovering that it can release creativity – because you cannot create out of nothing! Children who know no stories will not be able to create their own... the bigger the resource to draw upon, the more creative children can be.

Again and again, we have seen children's writing improve – often radically because at long last they have a story to tell. There have also been occasions when children with 'special needs' gain confidence and lead the class in storytelling. Progress can be startling.

If you want to know if it is working then record a few children before you start, asking them the question, 'Can you tell me a story?' After several weeks of storymaking ask the question again – and listen to the difference. Ideally – make a transcript so that you have evidence of progress to show anyone who asks! If the teaching is thorough and engaging, you will find that children move from having no tale to tell (or something rambling and disconnected) to being able to retell a whole story with fluency – and older pupils will add in their own variations to make it their own.

The process is simple enough. Soon it becomes an easy part of the everyday routine. Many schools now make sure that they build storytelling into their narrative units so that a year 6 class may read several short stories by Michael Morpurgo as well as working on an oral tale which will in the end act as a spine for their own creation. The impact can be quite dramatic – so keep at it!

Introduction

Let's create together schools, which have stories at their heart – for without them, we have heartless schools. It is worth remembering that at the heart of every culture lies song, dance, art, religion .... and stories. Without the arts, we have no heart, no culture and our schooling becomes dry dust upon the wind.

Chapter 1 Learning stories

The first stage (often referred to as 'imitation') is to help the children build up the bank of stories. This should be easy and quite natural – the teacher telling a story and the children gradually joining in until they know the story by heart – until the story is in their long-term working memory and will burn their like a flame forever.

Which story?

Choose a story that you enjoy and that you think the children will enjoy. I have provided a bank of well-known tales at the back of this book and suggested sources in the appendices. However, you may well be lucky enough to have children whose heritage is from other parts of the world and they or their families may also have other stories to share. As children move through the primary school, they need to acquire the most common traditional tales but also broaden this bank out to include tales from many other cultures. Without the common traditional tales from a culture, children cannot take part in that culture – they are cut off from one of the roots of that culture. Interestingly, children soon discover that every culture shares the same sorts of stories – because we are all human, similar patterns appear around the world.

Teaching the stories

The story that you have chosen will need to be told every day, possibly several times, using actions and a story map or board. The length of time it takes to learn a story varies – mature storymakers may only need a few days whilst young year three children may need several weeks of daily telling. Do not underestimate the importance of putting actions to help the tale along – especially including actions for the key connectives (see appendices for suggestions). Story maps are also essential as they provide a strong visual reminder so that the children can see the plot in one go. It is important to keep retelling the chosen story. The aim is to make sure that the story becomes burned into their memories.

Story maps

After you have told the story once then draw a story map or board in front of the children. The maps need to be simple and very clear so that they capture the plot in one go – and can act as a visual reminder. Remember to show on the map a simple pathway through the story – a dotted line or single line with an arrow should suffice.

The map needs to be on a large sheet of sugar paper and displayed at the front where it can be seen. Keep the map displayed while the children are learning the story. Ultimately, maps can be laminated and placed in a story map rack at the side of the room. These can then be used at any time for revisiting stories.

Once you have drawn the map and then used it for a second telling, it is worth the children drawing their own maps. Initially, children may just copy your map though more mature children can add extra words or images to help them recall the story. The act of having to reprocess the story and represent it in a different form helps to make the tale memorable in their minds. ... If you want children to remember something then the more they 'do' with it, in different ways, the more likely they will be to remember it.

Maps can be kept in a topic book of story maps or a writing journal that could move from year to year. After all, maps can be used at any level and revisited to create new stories.

Not all stories lend themselves to maps – though maps are good because they are so visual. You may need to use a storyboard, story mountain or flow chart. Whatever you do – provide a simple visual reminder, which will be very handy for those who think visually. Some teachers also use objects from the story such as puppets or pictures – all acting as visual prompts. This can be very useful for those for whom English is a new language. Though ultimately, you will want the children to 'imagine' and 'see' the story in their minds.

Actions

Whilst using story maps, objects or pictures helps to provide a visual prompt, actions that accompany the story also provide a kinaesthetic reminder that makes the language and tale more memorable as well as helping the children understand what is happening. Actions can be used to show events and are often made up by the children. However, the key connectives should have fixed actions so that in each class the children revisit connectives and build up a bank that they can call upon for their own storymaking.

It is worth reminding ourselves that language is not just words – it is also rhythm and action. If you watch a French speaker, you soon notice that the speech is accompanied by actions! Language and action are interlinked.

When telling stories, the children will be using typical narrative connectives *(Once upon a time, one day, first, next, after that, suddenly, finally)*. It is also handy if the teacher revisits some of the language features during the course of everyday classroom activities, e.g. *'This afternoon we have four things to do. First...., next....., after that.... Finally, we will have a story.....'*.

Whole class retelling – the communal story

Some teachers are worried that retelling the same story might become a bit boring. On one hand this may be so – but it is worth thinking about how much human beings like to revisit the same patterns. For instance, I have been listening to 'The Beatles' for over 30 years and still enjoy their songs. In a logical sense, this is ridiculous. I know what is going to happen; I know the songs word for word, note for note. So why is it that I keep on listening and enjoy hearing such familiar patterns?

Perhaps in order to survive, we need the comfort of patterning in our lives – otherwise the world would be a random blur of events. So – humans categorise, label and create patterns so that the world becomes something we understand and life is a series of routines and patterns without which we could not survive. Think how disturbing it can be when our daily routines are destroyed. Patterning is a fundamental comfort and coping device for humans. Narrative helps to provide basic patterns. Narrative is a template that we put upon life in order to explain our experiences to ourselves – and ourselves to the world.

You may find that after a while, you will want to ring the changes and find different ways to enliven and vary whole class retellings. Try the following ideas:

- all saying the story together;
- just girls or just boys;
- all those in blue/red/green...
- a group or pair lead the class;
- an individual sits in the teacher's 'storytelling' chair;
- a child leads the class wearing story cloak or hat;
- tell the story in different ways – loudly, softly, silently, just miming the actions, or very rapidly – babble gabble.

Withdrawing from telling

When you first tell a story to a class, you will be leading the way. Encourage the children to join in until they are saying every word with you. It is important that you then gradually withdraw from telling because you want the children to become independent. The more that you dominate the telling, the more that some children rely on you. Indeed, some children may never join in at all because you are doing all the work – they will just sit there passively, watching what you are doing.

However, this is not a 'performance' of story telling – the aim is for the children to learn the story. Once you have told it through several times, the children will begin to pick up on the most memorable parts – often the rhythmic, repetitive parts, the dialogue and the explosive dramatic bits. Keep going until the children are joining in with everything.

Once they seem confident, you can start to withdraw from saying the words – maybe you can just mouth the words or just keep prompting with the actions. If the children falter in their telling, you can always leap in and keep the story going. The aim is to move from you being the dominant teller to becoming a listener. The children move from being listeners to becoming tellers.

Teacher as teller	Withdraw and prompt	Teacher as listener
Children as listeners	Increasingly join in	Children as tellers

Story Circles

As the children become increasingly confident in telling the story in a whole class setting, you can move into story circles. The children sit in a small circle and try telling the story simultaneously. It is worth making sure that there is always an adult with story circles at the start to ensure that they do not loose their way. If they do not know the story well enough, they may slip into a string of sentences linked endlessly with 'and then'. The adult should not dominate the group but sit on the edge, ready to prompt if the children lose their way. Make sure too that the children can see their story maps.

Story Pairs

Only move to pairs, when you are fairly convinced that the children have the story in their long-term memory – this will take longer than you imagine. If you rush into pairs too quickly then the children will not know the story sufficiently well enough to retell it. Indeed, you may well have to stay at the level of whole class retelling until you have become pretty fed up with the story! The skill is for the teacher to dress up the whole class retelling in different ways – keeping it fun and lively.

Pairs can operate in three different ways. The first stage is for the children to retell together. They need to sit facing each other and stare into each other's eyes. They tell and perform the actions at the same time like a mirror. Their story maps could be placed on the ground in front of them. You will have to model how to work as a pair, showing them exactly what to do.

The second stage is for the tellers to take it in turns telling the story bit by bit. Often this will be sentence by sentence. A third stage is for the children to tell it in two halves – with the partner who is not telling ready to act as a prompt.

Pairs can be teamed up with pairs of children from other classes to retell their story. This provides an incentive and an audience for the retelling – after all, the point of learning a story is to tell it to someone else!

What about those who do not join in?

There are often a few children who do not join in. They sit on the carpet and just look at you – as if you had been beamed down from planet Zog! Look out for these children – the challenge will be to find ways to encourage them to participate. Are they actually internalising the story?

Sometimes this is just a lack of confidence and gradually, with plenty of encouraging smiles, they will join in. Some children may need reminding to join in. Others may need an adult to sit beside them and encourage them. Some may need to work in a smaller group or a pair with an adult. Often using puppets or finger puppets can help less confident children as the attention is taken away from the child and placed onto the puppet. You may well find that you have a child who has been worrying you – then one day Mum comes in and starts telling you how much they have been enjoying the retellings at home! Children who are learning English may begin by just following the actions – through constant repetition of a communal story they will begin to say the words as well.

Preparing to tell a story

The first time you tell a story without a book can be quite daunting. The usual panic is that you will forget the words – so solid preparation will pay off. Here are the basic steps:

1. Find your story.
    You could use a story from the bank in this book just to get you going or you may have a favourite of your own. Start with something simple so that you – and the children – gain confidence. Don't worry – the second story will be easier to learn – because you are exercising a part of the brain that you may not have used too often – also because you are developing memory and strategies for learning a chunk of text.

2. Adapt the story.
    I always rewrite the story. Partly because the rewriting helps me learn the tale – the act of reprocessing it through my brain and onto the page helps me to memorise it. But also because I want to build in certain sentence patterns and vocabulary (especially connectives) so that these are repeated enough to become part of the children's linguistic competence (see the language bank in the appendices).

3. Draw the map.
    I always draw a map before going anywhere near the classroom. This is important because it is not easy to come up with a simple, effective visual representation of a plot. The process of simplifying the story into its key incidents that will appear on the map also helps me to internalise the pattern of the tale (see appendices for an example).

4. Practice.
    I put the story onto a tape or burn it onto a cd so that I can play it in the car or on my Ipod. When I record the story, I do it line by line leaving a space in between each sentence. I make sure that the space is long enough for me to repeat the sentence. So – the recording teaches me. It says a sentence – I repeat it in the gap. As I begin to feel that I might know a bit – I turn off the recording and try saying it aloud. I keep doing this until I know it pretty well.

5. Build in actions.
    The final element is to make sure that I have thought through the actions. It is worth having certain actions that stay the same – the key connectives for example (see appendices for suggested actions). However, some actions can be made up with the class, providing ownership of the story.

Telling a story for the first time

This can be nerve wracking but once you have got over any initial qualms most people find storytelling enormous fun. Here are a few tips that may help you:

- have a map just beside you to glance at;
- pin a map on the wall behind the children so that if you get lost you can glance over the children's heads;
- have the script beside you to glance at;
- have the bare bones of the story on a prompt card;
- put the main scenes onto separate cards and then shuffle these as you tell, glancing at the card if you need prompting;
- put two classes together and tell the tale with a partner – one of you reading from the script.

Once you have told the story once – then you are fine. Because the next time the children will put you right... 'you didn't say that last time', is a very handy prompt! The truth is that after a while, you will have your own class version that you tell together and the story falls into its own pattern.

When you are telling a story, take time to settle children on the carpet – make sure that you can see everybody's eyes. As you tell the story, keep looking round, scanning the group and drawing them in with your eyes. Make your eyes larger and use expression. Vary the pace, using dramatic pauses as well as varying the volume. If anyone looks scared, tone the tale down. You may build in simple refrains or start with a short rhyme. Sometimes I use a musical instrument at the start and end – just to get everyone listening.

Getting going – the first story

The story of Little Charlie began life as 'Little Daisy' and then became 'Little Jack'. I invented it with help from Mary Rose as a first story to tell, building in specific patterns. It is a simple enough story to learn and can be innovated upon at a simple level by making a few changes or reused as a basic journey pattern and innovated upon at a more sophisticated level (see page 36).

Once upon a time there was a little boy called Charlie who lived on the edge of a big city.

Early one morning he woke up and his Mumma said, "Take this bag of goodies to your Grandma's." Into the bag she put – a slice of cheese, a loaf of bread and a square of chocolate.

Next he walked, and he walked and he walked till he came to a bridge. There he met a cat – a lean cat, a mean cat.
"I'm hungry," said the cat. "What have you got in your bag?"

"I've got a slice of cheese, a loaf of bread – but he kept the chocolate hidden!"
"I'll have the cheese please," said the cat. So Charlie gave the cheese to the cat and it ate it all up.

Next he walked, and he walked and he walked till he came to a pond. There he met a duck – a snowy white duck.
"I'm hungry," said the duck. "What have you got in your bag?"
"I've got a loaf of bread – but he kept the chocolate hidden!"
"I'll have the bread please," said the cat. So Charlie gave the bread to the duck and it ate it all up.

Next he walked, and he walked and he walked till he came to a tall town clock – tick tock, tick tock, tick tock. There he met not one, not two but three scruffy pigeons.
"We're hungry," said the pigeons. "What have you got in your bag?"
Unfortunately, there was only the chocolate – Luckily, Charlie found some crumbs. So he scattered them on the ground and the pigeons ate them all up.

Next he walked, and he walked and he walked till he came to a crossroads. There he met a .... Nobody.
"Mmmm, I'm hungry ," said Charlie. "What have I got in my bag?"
"Mmmmmm, chocolate!" So, he ate it all up!

Next he walked, and he walked and he walked till he came to Grandma's house. There he Grandma.
"I'm hungry ," said the Grandma. "What have you got in your bag?"
Unfortunately, there was only the chocolate wrapper – Luckily, grandma had pizza and chips for tea.

Understanding the story

Of course, chanting a story is one thing – indeed, if you are not careful a rhythmic chanting may actually be meaningless. The story needs to be told with expression and variation to bring it alive. If you are working with children for whom English is a new language or with those who might struggle with some of the vocabulary, then you may need extra prompts such as objects or pictures. This makes the learning of vocabulary simple, sensible and fun. Explaining what words mean is important.

Making it memorable

There are many different ways in which a story can be made memorable. Daily retelling is important but that in itself may not be sufficient for some children – especially those who do not learn so powerfully in an auditory manner.

Learning stories

Given a story such as the 'Jack and the Beanstalk', most teachers can begin to generate a suite of activities that might help to make the tale memorable as well as capitalising on the children's interests – growing beans, making a large wall map of the journey, hot seating the characters, writing a diary entry by Jack, interviewing the giant's wife who has just been robbed, painting pictures and making models all spring to mind as possibilities. It is worth asking ourselves – what are the key activities that really help the children internalise the story? Of course, other activities may well spring out of the story and be part of the broader curriculum.

Generally speaking, the more you do with a story – the more it is reprocessed in the mind in different ways, the more memorable it becomes. It is worth devising a multi-sensory programme so that they children have activities that open each channel for learning as well as opportunities to 'play' at the story: -

Visual – map, storyboard, flow chart, paint, draw, model and watch the story;

Auditory – hear and say the story, discussing, retelling, drama;

Cognitive – memory tricks, discussions, key connectives;

Kinaesthetic – drama, role-play, dance, model making, building.

Think **VACK** when planning, making sure that you have built in opportunities for stories to be represented through art in a visual manner, through drama in a kinaesthetic way as well as retelling and thinking about the story.

Providing an audience for the story

In the hurly burly of learning the story, it is easy to lose sight of the whole purpose of storytelling – to communicate a story to someone else. It is always worth building into the programme of activities some sort of chance to retell to a new audience: –

- whole class assembly performance;
- capture the story on video/digital camera and show to other classes on interactive board;
- class, group or paired retelling to other classes;
- make a CD of retellings and sell to community.

Some classes use a mini recorder as a regular part of their storymaking. The children learn a story and then retell their version into the recorder. This means that they can listen to their own retelling – which has the result of the children hearing their own telling –becoming their own audience. It becomes a simple way of assisting oral redrafting.

Learning stories

Story boxes, museums and puppets

This can be quite a fun activity but also acts as a powerful visual representation of a story. The boxes can simply contain objects from the story. Your boxes could be simple shoeboxes – decorated – and inside will be your story items. Or the boxes can have two sides cut off so that a simple 'room' or scene can be created using small items of doll's furniture, etc.

The story museum is a similar idea. The class collect objects from the story as well as images, photos, video clips, sound effects and create a story museum that follows the pattern of the story as it is told. The museum can be set out in the hall for others to visit. Large puppets, finger and stick puppets are all part of the storymaking classroom. These provide a real stimulus for retelling to an audience.

Drama and storytelling

Drama is a natural accompaniment to storymaking. It helps children get to know the text really well – often having to listen again to and reuse parts of the text. Drama activities are especially useful for encouraging a return to the original story to internalise the patterns and develop an interpretation.... Also, drama can help children begin to generate new ideas for their own inventions.

- **Teacher in role** – in this way you can introduce problems, add depth, or keep the drama together, maintaining the pace and deepen belief. Often you will be an authority figure or messenger bringing news to add to the drama.
- **Pupil in role – role playing** – scenes or alternative events – this can be very effective for 'innovation' – to help children embellish a scene.
- **Free role play** – providing a play area complete with dressing up clothes acts as a simple invitation to 'play at' the story.
- **Hot seating** and **freeze frames.**
- **Miming scenes** – miming a scene from a story. Can the others guess which scene? Miming what might happen next.
- **Meetings** – hold a meeting to discuss what has happened in role as villagers and what next.
- **Act the story** – in this the teacher, possibly with the main body of the class – retells the story and a group act the story out. This can be followed by children working in groups to re-enact the story, using a narrator.
- **Puppet theatre** – finger puppets and a mini theatre should be used for children to play at the story – retelling it or inventing new ideas using the same characters.
- **Journalists** – interviewing the characters about what has happened.
- **'News' programmes** – complete with outside broadcasting unit – TV or radio – e.g. interview with Troll about threatening behaviour of local vandals.

- **Monologues** – begin this by drawing an outline of the character's head and asking for ideas about what the character might be thinking or feeling. Demonstrate how to be in role as a character and 'think aloud' the 'thoughts in the head'. This might be a character in a story or a character that is not mentioned, e.g. the wolf's wife might be very fed up with his behaviour.... 'He's always huffing and puffing up and down the den. I just don't know what is wrong with him...'
- **Gossip** – between characters about events. These could be main characters but using bystanders can be handy as a way of revisiting what has happened – a form of retelling, e.g. a neighbour of the bears could tell a friend all about the break in.
- **Mobile phone calls** – from a character to an off stage character provides another ideal form of recounting events from a different viewpoint.
- **Advice surgeries or working in role as agony aunts** – this provides a chance to work with the main character, digging under the skin of what they have been doing, why – considering motive. The advice might suggest other ways forward for a story.
- **Statements to police** – what does the wolf have to say about his behaviour?
- **Drawing/writing in role** – drawing scenes, maps, creating documents – there are many possibilities for writing in role that help the children revisit the story, e.g. end of term report for a character, diary entry, letters to another character, newspaper articles.
- **Objects or costumes** – telling the tale of the character, or placing the object in the centre to then decide what should happen, e.g. a baby's rattle is placed in the centre of the group as part of work on the workhouse in Victorian Britain. The baby has been abandoned – what should happen? Use costume to generate thinking – about a character, e.g. use buttons, scrap torn from a coat, contents of a pocket.
- **Forum theatre** – a scene is set up. The action can be paused and audience members suggest what might happen next.
- **Re-enacting key scenes** – e.g. the moment when jack breaks into the giant's kitchen.
- **Trials** – teacher in role as judge. Children work as solicitors to defend or accuse a character, e.g. the Iron Man for wrecking the countryside. Characters from the story can be called to explain what has happened.
- **Role on the wall** – someone lies down on sheets of paper – an outline is drawn plus comments, quotes, and suggestions.
- **Thoughts in the head** – e.g. work in pairs – one child says aloud what they are thinking having walked past an old house. Then their partner role-plays the old person who lives in the house.

Learning stories not 'word for word'

Learning stories 'by heart' in a communal fashion where the class chant the tale together is a handy way to gather confidence, support each other and to establish patterns of narrative in the mind. You will find that a few easy stories learned in this way will be very handy. Indeed, those who struggler or are new to English should learn communal stories possibly for a year or

Learning stories

two. If you look in the Bumper Book of Storytelling Key Stage 1, you will find the year 2 stories (and some year 1) will suit strugglers and give them great confidence. Stories such as 'The Little Red Hen' have been used with older pupils in special needs settings with great success.

However, as children become confident tellers you may wish to move into learning the stories not 'word for word' so that the children begin to develop their own slightly different versions right from the start. Begin by telling the story – or at a pinch you could listen to a recorded version though this is not so powerful.

Choose something relatively simple. Listen to the tale and discuss. Then retell it and ask the children to draw a story map. Have a look at suggested maps together with children talking through the basic plot.

Then ask the children to work in pairs and work out the main scenes – this can be done by 'walking the story steps' where the children take a step for each new scene – or by drawing a story flow chart – a box for each scene. So the story of Icarus might have the following main scenes:

Minos is angry because Daedalus
made the labyrinth for his son the Minotaur.

He imprisons Daedalus and Icarus in a tower

Daedalus collects materials to make wings

They fly from the prison

Daedalus warns Icarus not to fly too high

Icarus flies too high

The wings melt and he falls into the sea.

Come together as a class and agree on the key scenes. This can be drawn as a flow chart of storyboard. Already you can see that you have begun to develop what might ultimately become a series of paragraphs.

Let the children use their flow chart to have a go at retelling the tale. They will borrow much from the original retelling but can 'say it in their own way'. Instantly, they will begin to add and alter and develop the tale.

Now spend time working on their retelling. As they work on different aspects of their story, ask them to record in their journals – and then retell their story dropping in the new developments. In this way they keep retelling and refining and embellishing their tale. In the end when they move into writing, they will have developed their own tale – but also, they will have spent time improving their story. They will be motivated to write – and you have also made the act of writing easier because they do not have to make up what to say at the same time as struggling to get it down upon the page by releasing a chunk of cognitive space. You may wish to ask them to work on the following:

Opening – develop a dramatic opening or a question to draw the listener into the tale. This can be noted down and used in telling but also stored up for writing.

Characterization – look at each scene in turn and decide how the main character feels. Practise showing this by think about what they do – use powerful verbs to help show feelings and rehearse sentences aloud.

Dialogue – take each scene in turn. Ask the class to invent the dialogue – thinking about how the characters feel and therefore what they might say. Work orally first and then note down the dialogue. Think about the speech verbs as well as 'stage direction' – adding on what the character is doing as they speak, e.g. *'Do not fly too high,' snapped Daedalus, as he climbed onto the window ledge.*

Atmosphere – take each section again and decide on the mood of the passage – is this suspense, sad, excited, ... Try sentences out to create the mood and build into the tale.

Description – again, take each scene. Invent and note down a few specific details of description, think about what needs to be described. Again, retell the tale adding in the new descriptive elements.

Dilemma – spend time working on the most dramatic moment, deploying short punchy sentences and building the drama.

Ending – make sure that the ending is satisfying and shows what has been learned or how the main character has changed.

Between each focus it is worth hearing examples told aloud – not the whole tale – but specific sentences or a section. What can be learned from the other children? Build up lists of useful tactics – and keep these available on a wall chart or noted in children's writing journals. Remember to encourage children top re-use old strategies, borrow from tales they have previously heard or read as well as magpie from each other.

Making storytelling special

There are a number of simple 'extras' that help to create a storymaking classroom. Displays are obvious – but what about:

- **Storyteller's hat** – a fancy hat for telling.
- **Storyteller's chair** – dress up the chair.
- **Storyteller's cloak** – velvet and shimmering stars!
- **Magic carpet** – a flight to story world.
- **Story music –** to establish atmosphere (CDs of music from films can be handy).

- **Story lights** – a star shape or crescent moon.
- **Story box or bag** – for puppets or secret objects.

Discussing the story

A key factor in helping children understand the story will be discussing what happens. Questioning is important and it does help if this does not sink to the level of the teacher firing comprehension questions like some sort of verbal reasoning test. The phrase 'tell me' as an invitation to discuss reading was first introduced to me by Aidan Chambers in his excellent book titled 'Tell Me' (Thimble Press). Begin by asking the children to 'tell you' what they liked, disliked, any puzzles or patterns. These four areas will often open up some discussion between the children. Make sure that you show interest in the children's ideas so that you model being a good listener.

It is also worth being aware of the importance of asking questions that do not just rely on simple retrieval and description. Move on to questions that involve deduction and inference – perhaps asking how someone might have felt where it is not obviously stated in the text. Of course, drama activities such as hot seating all help to deepen children's understanding of a story by putting them into different character's shoes. To add extra depth, try coupling a told story with several written stories.

Daily retelling

I cannot stress enough the importance of retelling the story daily. You do not have to make a great fuss and a do about this but memorable repetition is very important in language learning. If you drop the process for a while because Christmas has struck then don't blame me if the children struggle!

Revisiting old favourites

Every now and then, revisit an old favourite. The idea is for the children to acquire a cumulative bank of tales – the first is not lost. By the time we reach the summer term, we have a bank of 6 or so stories that we know well.

Storytime

Some teachers have moved on to holding a special 'storytime' every day. This can be very helpful in schools where language learning is an issue. 'Storytime' might last about half an hour and consists of different aspects of story. It might include such activities as: –

- read the next chapter from the class novel;
- read a new picture book, short story to the class and discuss;
- reread an old favourite;
- sing an action rhyme;
- read a new poem or old chestnut;
- whole class retelling of an old favourite;
- retell story being learned;
- teacher makes up a new story with suggestions from the children.

Poems and rhymes

Sadly, there are many children who only know a smattering of poems – if any. Poem of the day is a simple idea. Once a week the teacher reads the poem – on the other days, children take their turn. This could be solo or with friends. The Macmillan anthologies (The Works or Read Me) provide plenty of child friendly material. 'The Works Key Stage 2' (edited by Pie Corbett) provides a bank that is organised by year group.

Parents

Involving parents in storymaking is the next obvious step for any storymaking class or school. There are many different ways in which this might occur. Many schools now have banks of tapes, CDs and story sacks that can be borrowed and used at home. They also hold sessions for parents and carers to learn about sharing books with children. This is something that we have to keep at relentlessly – every new batch of children brings a new group of parents. I well recall one parent who attended a session about the importance of reading to children, saying afterwards that she wished she had known this for her first child.

Story telling workshops, where parents are taught how to tell stories, would be useful. These could be lead by teachers or where possible by community members, so that different groups can learn stories from different communities, enriching everyone's story storehouse. Stories could also be put onto tapes, or CDs – either by an adult or by children. These might be handy for car journeys – or last thing at night.

Parents and carers too need to know how to build up a bank of 'family' stories as well as traditional tales – those stories about things that have happened in a family. Stories about trips, relatives and things that happen in everyday life... *'Tell us the story about when we...'*

A storymaking school

A storymaking school would have a strong commitment to reading, writing, performing – there would be storymaking areas and every class would have magical mats, hats, cloaks... there might be a story giant's chair in the playground or a mini forum for performance....

there would be story maps and everywhere you go – children telling stories or watching performances. Drama and puppet groups would be a regular occurrence and so too would visits from authors. There would be homemade books by classes and children. Projects would spring out of stories. Narrative would be a living thing – central to children's lives.

If we are to genuinely help children develop their story writing then we cannot underestimate the importance of reading to the class on a daily basis and encouraging children to read more at home. It is worth remembering that if we do not read to them – then many children will never be read to. Also – if they do not hear language being used beautifully then how can we expect them to use language beautifully? As one teacher in Southampton said to me, 'I've learned that stories do not just fly into the head ready formed from nowhere!'

Stories provide children with the equipment with which to create their own tales.... And ultimately, storytelling can help raise standards. But is also develops the imagination, passes on culture and values as well as developing the ability to think in the abstract.

Chapter 2 Changing stories

The second stage in storymaking is where you take a well-known story and change it a bit to make it your own (often called 'innovation). This is a traditional approach to storymaking that has gone on for thousands of years. For instance, Shakespeare wrote 39 plays.... and only 3 of them were original, the rest were all innovations on well-known tales!

In the main, nearly all writing in primary schools is 'innovation' – you can usually spot the underlying patterns.... In fact, if I look back at the stories that I was writing when I was about ten years old, it was pretty obvious what I was reading – all my stories involved 3 children and a dog named scamp – holiday, cave, treasure, nasty villain appears, hide, police at last moment, steaming mug of cocoa and reward. The end. Yes – I was an Enid Blyton innovator!

Actually, as you become more used to looking at the underlying patterns in narratives, you begin to notice how the same sorts of patterns reoccur. Indeed, many people would suggest that there are only a few patterns constantly recycled. Christopher Hampton in 'The Seven Basic Plots' suggests there are only seven. We will return to this idea when we look at the third stage of 'invention'.

It is worth bearing in mind that the idea of 'innovation' is based on how children learn language. Initially, they imitate the sound patterns that they hear repetitively used in certain contexts. This is often rewarded by the parents' delight so they repeat the 'word' again. As the child builds a vocabulary, innovations appear. The most obvious example is the way in which young children generalise the past tense principle and add 'ed' on where it doesn't quite work – I 'goed' down the lane. When children innovate, it is a sign of language growth – the brain has generalised the principle and is trying to apply it into new situations.

It is worth reminding ourselves at this point that it is important not to move on to innovation until the original story is well embedded within the children's long-term working memory. With communal, chanted stories, the yardstick for this is whether they can retell it independently. If you move on too quickly then the results will disappoint. The teacher has to beware of the curriculum's desire to encourage you to dash on, 'delivering' objectives with scant regard for whether anyone has learned anything. Storymaking schools have learned that for many children slowing down and learning thoroughly through imaginative repetition is a surer way of securing genuine progress. When children are experienced story makers they may only need to hear a well told version several times for them to begin to develop their own version.

Innovation is harder than imitation – at first! It really has to be taught.... the quality of the children's innovations is a direct reflection of the quality of the teacher's innovation. There are 5 basic possibilities – though often these intermingle.

1. **substitution** – making simple changes;
2. **addition** – retelling the same story but adding in more. Most stories can be embellished up to a level 5!;

3. **alteration** – retelling the same story but making significant changes that have repercussions;
4. **change of viewpoint** – retelling the same story but from a different angle;
5. **recycling the plot** – reusing the underlying plot and theme but in a totally different context.

These five stages are hierarchical – in so far as they become increasingly sophisticated. Most year 3 strugglers will be able to accomplish a simple 'substitution' but by the end of the year may well be adding in some extra description or events.

However, a confident year three class may well be altering events, adding in much more description or even retelling a tale from a different character's viewpoint. They might reuse the underlying plot to create a totally new story.

The beauty of this approach is that it makes differentiation easier. Some children in a year 3 class will be retelling with a few simple substitutions – whilst others may be adding in detail or making significant alterations. What is essential is that the teacher ensures that ultimately the children's compositions are supported by the original telling but also allow them to make progress. A confident year three should not just be doing a simple substitution! Let us take a closer look at the five categories: -

1. Substitutions

This is the easiest form of innovation. A few simple changes can provide a sense of ownership and accomplishment for the youngest and least confident. For those who are learning English, substitution provides a simple way of deploying new vocabulary within sentences.

Usually, places, characters and names are substituted. One word of warning though – some children are tempted to substitute too much and then find that they cannot recall all the changes so the plot... literally... falls apart! It may be worth limiting or staging the substitutions so that you gain success. Model how to change a story by redrawing or changing the class map and using this for telling of the new version.

So, a simple substitution for 'Little Charlie' might start like this:

One upon a time there was a little girl called Josie who lived on the edge of a big forest.

Early one morning her Dad woke her up and said, 'Take this basket of food to your Auntie's house.' Into the bag he put a ripe banana, a slice of chocolate cake and an apple.....

2. Additions

In some ways making additions comes quite naturally. Children retelling a story will often start adding extra bits in the same way that in conversation when they are telling about things that have happened, they may embellish for an audience ... so the tale grows in the telling...

The simplest way to move into addition is by adding in more description, e.g.

Early one frosty morning Charlie woke up. He ran over to the window and stared out at the snow on the roads.......

You could build on this by:

- adding in more dialogue;
- adding in a new character -
- adding in new incidents -

Usually, you will find that you are not only adding extra events or description but also substituting as well. Keep demonstrating how to add and embellish.

As the children become experienced spend more time on embellishing, developing and refining their tale. This can be done by working out the main scenes into a simple flow chart. Then work on separate elements of the story in a focussed way, retelling sections as you go along. Use a simple chart to note ideas down as they are orally developed:

Scene	Dialogue
Jack meets the giant's wife	"And who are you?" asked the giant's wife, as she leaned down to peer at Jack.

You could focus on:

Opening – develop a dramatic opening or a question to draw the listener into the tale.

Characterization – look at each scene in turn and decide how the main character feels.

Dialogue – take each scene in turn. Ask the class to invent the dialogue – thinking about how the characters feel and therefore what they might say.

Atmosphere – try sentences out to create the mood and build into the tale.

Description – invent and note down a few specific details of description, think about what needs to be described.

Dilemma – spend time working on the most dramatic moment, deploying short punchy sentences and building the drama.

Ending – make sure that the ending is satisfying and shows what has been learned or how the main character has changed.

3. Alterations

Of course, a substitution is a form of alteration. However, most simple substitutions have little consequence. By 'alteration' I mean a change that is significant and changes the direction of the tale – alterations have a knock on effect!

It is worth beginning by just making changes within the story – so that the children have the overall comfort of the original, to act as a large writing frame and provide a structure within which they can manoeuvre. You could try altering:

- the nature of one or more of the characters, e.g. the giant is afraid of heights;
- settings, e.g. put Jack onto a modern estate;

Many teachers like to alter the ending of the story – because children find endings difficult. Thinking up new ways to end the story, twisting the tale in a different direction helps to build up a store of possibilities for the children to draw upon when they are creating. So teachers often focus upon:

- altering the way the story opens or ends;
- altering dialogue;
- building suspense;
- rehearsing action;
- developing the resolution;
- considering how a character changes across a story;
- showing how a character feels by what they say or do.

Another common approach is to alter a key event within the tale or add in some new ones as a result. I remember hearing a year two girl retelling the gingerbread man in which the man got seized by a hungry girl called Gretel and eaten up! It was a lovely example of one tale wandering into another but did rather surprise all the characters that were chasing the gingerbread man!

4. Change of Viewpoint

This is far more sophisticated than a basic retelling with additions and changes. The children have to see the story from another angle. Plenty of drama and lots of modelling by the teacher can help the children into changes of viewpoint. There are two key ways to do this:

- retell a tale from the viewpoint of another character;
- retell a tale as a different text type, e.g. as a diary entry, letter or news report.

Changing stories

Seeing things from a different viewpoint is enhanced by activities such as hot seating. The teacher writing in role or talking in role about what has happened also helps. Providing opportunities for role-play will also allow the children to step into different roles. It is fascinating to ask the children to retell a tale with different children working from the different characters' viewpoints, e.g. the giant's wife, the giant, Jack's mother, Jack and a villager.

Re-cycle the basic plot

Finally, we come to the idea of just re-using the underlying pattern, plot or theme and totally rewriting the story. So, 'the Gingerbread Man' is a story about a wrong doer who is chased but meets a well-deserved end! 'The Billy Goats Gruff' is a journey story in which there is a barrier to overcome. Or 'Goldilocks' is a tale about someone who enters a forbidden place and breaks, ruins or steals something of value only to be faced with the 'owner' or guardian! It's a 'break and entry' story that could be re-written as a spy story. Little Charlie is based on the underlying pattern of Lord of the Rings and could be rewritten as a space story with Captain Zarg taking medical supplies and a secret message to the planet Tharg....

Re-using the basic plot means that you can start with a traditional tale but reset it as a science fiction, detective or any other genre. The original tale just provides the plot pattern and theme.

Moving the telling into writing

Do not consider asking the children to write until they have a story to tell. Many may fail if you ask them to create a story on the hoof as they write.... thorough preparation will provide success – progress and motivation. Everyone will start with an oral substitution – some may proceed further. Let's see if we can map out a rough idea of how the storymaking process will run – bearing in mind that there may well be variations that you discover work.

Story Innovation Process

1. Tell the new story with actions.
2. Draw a story map or storyboard.

3. Retell the story daily

4. Move onto story circles and pairs as well as whole class.

5. As the children internalise the story into their long-term working memory – begin innovation.
6. Work on different aspects of the story, bit by bit, e.g. adding description.
7. Keep retelling the new version, adding new elements.

8. Teacher leads the children through creating their innovation.
9. Children draw their new map and retell their innovation.

10. Teacher demonstrates shared writing of class innovation.
11. Pupils write or record their own innovations.
12. Polishing and publishing of stories.

This process allows for success. The children only move on to the writing when they really do have something to say. Often when children are asked to write, they struggle because there is too much happening inside their minds. They have to orchestrate too many things – the pencil grip, spellings, where does the dot go... let alone what to say. If some of the writing processes are not easy and automatic, the brain is overloaded and there is insufficient cognitive space for composition. Weaker writers will worry about handwriting and spelling and this intervenes and cuts out the ability to compose – indeed, it just makes writing laborious, painful and dull. No wonder so many start fidgeting and fooling about!

However, if when you sit down to write you really have a story to tell then the child is not only more motivated to write but also will find it easier because it has released a large chunk of cognitive space.

Now this all sounds well and good but..... we have been putting a lot of effort into developing the compositional side of writing – what about the transcriptional skills? These too need attention and developing.

- Handwriting – lots of work on fine and gross motor skills leading into regular handwriting practice – for young children this may be daily.
- Spelling – daily phonics and spelling work;
- Sentences – daily sentence games to develop the ability to compose and manipulate sentences. I have described sentence and spelling games in 'Jumpstart Literacy' published by David Fulton. I cannot emphasise enough the need to practise saying and writing sentences swiftly and fluently and accurately, the sentence is essential to writing – it is as important as kicking is to football. Children who cannot write sentences cannot write whole texts – daily practice will pay dividends. Especially if you build into the

games 'progress' so they practise the sorts of sentences and language features that will help them improve their writing.

In the same way that right at the start of the storymaking process the teacher needs to identify the key spellings that will ultimately be needed to write the story and to practise or provide those, we also need to think about the sorts of sentences that will be needed.

These sentences need to be practised daily so that when the children come to write, the act of writing will be easier – they have been well prepared. This may mean practising 'suddenly' sentences, 'once upon a time' sentences, 'adverb starters' and so on. In particular, it is worth practising making up sentences using different connectives that vary their openings and vary the sentence type.

If children have not heard how a connective is used in a sentence then there is no chance that they will somehow be able to magically do this on their own. They need plenty of practice 'hearing' how a complex sentence works and then 'saying' them.... as well as reading and writing them. But the 'hearing' and 'saying' must come first.

Certain stories will throw up obvious sentence types to rehearse. But also consider what will help the children make progress – in year three, they will need to begin varying sentences, handling compound and complex sentences, using a variety of connectives, varying openings, using interesting vocabulary.... and all this needs daily practice.

If the children are uncertain then you will need to model orally and then in writing – demonstrating and then asking for contributions. Once they become confident, you can move to practising on mini whiteboards. Good sentences can be stored for future use in their writing journals

If you look in the appendix, you will find the 'language bank' that identifies key aspects of language such as connectives and sentence variation to teach each year. These can embedded into the stories you work on but will also need regular practice.

Try beginning sessions with spelling games, followed by sentence games. This will need to be well organised, otherwise you will eat into the main body of the session. Most of the games can be done orally though with more confident writers you will want to use mini whiteboards. Some of the games lend themselves to using words and parts of sentences on strips of card to make the game more tactile and visual – rather like a maths washing line. You could also use an interactive whiteboard. Anyway, here are the main games in brief – though you will also have others that may be handy.

● *Sentence Builder*

In this game you give the children one word (*dog*) and the children have to make up a sentence using that word (*I saw an old dog running along*). Once they are confident with this, move to two words (*cat/jumped – the angry cat jumped onto the table*). In the end you might get as far as three words and introduce using connectives (*dog barked because – the dog barked because the cat stole its bone*).

If the children cannot rapidly make up a sentence then they will not be able to write whole texts so this is an important skill. Try it orally and in writing. When inventing sentences orally ask the children to put in the punctuation using an action and sound. This shows you that they know that there should be a full stop and it acts as a really good learning device to remind them. Be ruthless on insisting on full stops orally and in writing right from the start – get those footballs in!

● *Boring sentences*

In this game you write up a really dull sentence (or paragraph for the more confident) and the children have to 'improve' it. This could be done in various ways. Take the sentence.

The dog went down the road.

This doesn't actually build a very powerful picture in the reader's mind and could be improved. You could:

1. Change words – *The Alsatian limped down the High Street.*
2. Add words in – *The shaggy dog went carefully down the deserted road.*
3. Add words on – *The dog went down the road because the cat had bitten its tail.*

Remember the following:

- ▣ watch out for weak nouns as well as verbs ('ostrich' not just 'bird');
- ▣ don't just add in adjectives – collect a bag of adverbs and get using them;
- ▣ add on by using a connective at the end of the sentence and for mature writers get them adding on at the start (*Because the pet shop had been broken into, the dog went down the road...*).

It is worth also introducing children to using:

- ▣ alliteration – repeating a sound close together – *Sam the serious seal ate cereal slowly...*;
- ▣ simile using 'like' – *broccoli is like moss*;
- ▣ simile using 'as' – *as thin as an eyelash.*

● *Sentence Doctor*

This game is about spotting mistakes. Feed off the children's common errors so that they get used to spotting the sort of thing that they often get wrong – then they can move on to simple response partnering and looking for their own errors as well as places to improve. Write up sentences that have mistakes – spellings, missing words, punctuation errors, shifts in tenses, incorrect use of pronouns, etc.

● *Drop in*

This can become a simple part of the children's 'polishing' (editing) routine – where they get used to re-reading their work to find places where they can 'drop in' words. The game is to provide them with a sentence and they drop in words. Remember to encourage adverbs as well as adjectives. Also – watch out for the overuse of adjectives as this can make the writing worse!

You could try a game called 'shorten' – which involves giving the children an over-written sentence to shorten – or play a game called 'lengthen' in which you give them a very short sentence that they have to make longer!

● *Join it*

This is a very important game and worth playing in year two on many occasions. The idea is to provide the children with two short simple sentences that relate to each other chronologically. The children then have to join them using a connective (not 'and' or 'then' – because we know the children can use those two!).

The door opened.
The princess came out.

Now the children have to make one sentence by using a connective either between the sentences or at the front, e.g.

As the door opened, the princess came out.
The door opened as the princess came out.

Words that would work well here include:

As, as soon as, after, before, although, immediately, when, whenever, while, so, because, but.

● *Imitation*

In this game you simply model a type of sentence that you want the children to use and then they have to innovate on the pattern. For instance, you might show year 2 children how to do an adverb starter (*Slowly, she crept along*) and then use a bag of adverbs to invent their own 'adverb starters'.

- ## *Punctuating stories*

  Getting into the habit of putting in a full stop can be very hard. After all, when we speak and read punctuation does not make a sound. It does very little that is memorable. If you have many children who find this a challenge, a simple but effective tactic is to introduce 'sound punctuation' in year one. Perhaps during the second term where the writing is beginning to flow, learn several stories in the normal way but for every punctuation mark add in a sound effect and action. This makes great fun and also more importantly, it makes the punctuation memorable. You will see that when they write the story down, they are more likely to use punctuation. Have a go at this – it works like magic! Also try a game where you read sentences and put in the sounds and actions for the punctuation.

- ## *Final thoughts on sentences*

  For many children talking and writing in whole sentences does not come easily because they have not had sufficient experience of hearing and saying sentences. It is vital that this is addressed in a vigorous and focussed manner because if the brain does not acquire sentence patterns early on, it can become too late and in extreme cases of deprivation there are children who will never be able to acquire syntax. Sentence acquisition comes through modelling, reflecting and extending children's responses – and plenty of reading, composing, playing and talking.

Modelling writing

In the same way that children can learn a story orally through imitation so too children can learn how to write by imitation. Every opportunity should be taken to model writing. We have to show children how to plan, write and then edit or polish their writing – making simple improvements and ensuring accuracy.

Certainly, before the children write their story down, the teacher will be writing up the class innovation in front of the children. This is a key strategy for drawing upon all sorts of aspects of teaching – handwriting, spelling, and punctuation through to using good words. When the teacher is 'modelling' or 'demonstrating', it is worth trying to provide a 'running commentary', explaining what you are doing. For instance, it is important to demonstrate how to:

- say the sentence to yourself (rehearsal);
- write it down;
- reread what you have written.

Re-reading is important. Firstly, because you need to check that you have written what you intended to write. Secondly, it provides the link into making up the next sentence. Finally, more mature writers might think of a way of improving or 'polishing' what has been written – by adding in or changing words for instance. Make it obvious when you are referring to word lists or using specific words or sentences that you have been practising. In the main, 'modelling' or 'demonstration' is used to show children:

- new things, e.g. a new text type;
- hard things, e.g. dialogue;
- progress – things that if the children use them, they will make progress, e.g. using a variety of connectives.

When you are setting about modelling, it is important to be clear what it is that you will specifically be demonstrating – the aspect of progress that you are emphasising or teaching.

Shared Writing

Shared writing is when the children are joining in – the truth is that very often some of the time you are deciding what happens but also young children will want to make suggestions. Keep challenging and also maintain the pace. I have seen some miserably slow writing sessions where we have ended up with several sentences up on the board after having spent a lot of time sounding each word out. Then the children went off and wrote several pages! It's a shame if the teacher cannot write as well as the children!

What you end up with on the board needs to be just above where the majority of the children are. If most are at about level three – then you need to show them level four!

It is also worth writing up whole stories and not just openings. Children need to see every aspect of a story modelled. Many teachers spread a story out over a week so that the class focus on a different 'section' or 'scene' each day.

Writing journals

Writing journals are very handy as a resource for children. The journals contain all the useful reminders and lists and models that we use with the children. It might contain things like 'words to use instead of 'said' as well as story maps, spelling lists for specific stories or pieces of non-fiction. For instance, under 'recounts' there might be a handy list of connectives such as 'first, next, after that, later on, finally'.

Children could get used to noticing in their reading useful words or writing tactics and borrowing these to use in their own telling and writing. In this way the idea of 'writers are thieves' begins to make sense – being alert to how other writers create effects and then reusing the same strategies.

Chapter 3 Making up stories

The third aspect of storymaking is children making up stories on their own (often known as 'invention'). Of course, to do this they have to draw upon their bank of stories, as well as their general experience of life, things that have happened to them, stories read and seen as well as new ideas that they think of for themselves – new possibilities.

The specific phase of 'invention' can be moved into as the children build up a bank of known narratives – certainly once several stories have been learned you can begin to successfully make stories up together because already fundamental patterns – 'story pathways' – have been laid down in the brain.

In many year three classes, you might consider holding regular weekly story inventing sessions. You could invent stories with the whole class, groups, pairs or individuals. The basic approach is to make up a story orally – initially without the fuss of writing it down. The teacher guides the process – though over time it is important that the children become increasingly involved and independent until in the end they can invent stories for themselves. This means that the teacher has to 'withdraw' from dominating and shaping the story invention sessions.

When inventing a new story, it is useful to reuse familiar characters, settings, events and patterns as well as encouraging new ideas. Keep reusing connectives, sentences and story patterns to help link ideas together and provide underlying structures for their creations. For instance – once the teacher is armed with a simple set of connectives then a story becomes possible –

Once upon a time....

One day.....

Unfortunately....

Luckily.....

Finally.....

All this should ideally appear seamless and natural to the children with the teacher lending a guiding hand.

Starting Points

It is worth experimenting and building up a range of different strategies to encourage the invention of stories. Here are some possibilities: –

- making up another story about a favourite character from a story or picture book;
- make up a story about an unusual object;
- reuse a familiar plot pattern;
- hide items in a box or bag for a character to find;
- use a set of character and settings cards to choose 'who' and 'where';

Making up stories

- give the 'baddie' a negative characteristic – sad, lonely, angry, mean, spiteful, foolish, cunning, sly...;
- give the main character a characteristic – clever, brave, hungry, lonely, hopeful, careful, kind, generous, happy...;
- use a set of dilemma cards to choose something that goes wrong;
- take a simple picture book like 'Pig in the Pond' or 'Owl Babies' and retell in new setting with new characters;
- Choose a basic theme for the story, e.g.
    a. Helping someone
    b. Mistaken identity
    c. Feeling afraid
    d. Surprises
    e. Getting in trouble
    f. Sad – happy
    g. Alone – friendship
    h. Wrong – right
    i. Silly – wise
    j. Mean – generous
- Music played – time to day dream, to close your eyes and begin to 'see' a story;
- Pictures to observe – what happened before, during and next;
- Posters of paintings with something happening;
- Video clips or stills;
- Still images on the screen ordered to create or suggest a plot;
- Writing extra incidents around a known tale;
- Intriguing objects – a shiny button, a lantern, an old map, a key;
- Places – inventing on location – what happened here?
- Teacher in role – telling their story;
- A letter arrives, half a secret message is discovered;
- Drama – acting out and creating a story together.

Whole class inventions

Remember that when you are making up stories with children, you do not need anything complicated – KEEP IT SIMPLE. Try to avoid inventing a rambling, complex tale than that does not act as a simple model for the children.

Settle the children down and introduce the stimulus or starting point. Then just scaffold their ideas as the tale unfolds:

'Once upon a time there was – shall we have a girl, boy or maybe an animal this time? – a fox! – ok – let's start again – Once upon a time there was a fox called – what should we call the fox? – Kirk! – Once upon a time there was a fox called Kirk who lived... now where did he live....?'

Making up stories

In your mind keep a simple story frame to guide the story and it will give you confidence:

- ◾ Introduce a character in a setting – *'once upon a time there was.... who lived ....'*
- ◾ Get them doing something or going somewhere – *'one day....'*
- ◾ Something goes wrong – *'unfortunately....'*
- ◾ Sort it out – *'luckily...'*
- ◾ Have a good ending – *'happily ever after'*.

The basic plots

The more that I have discussed stories with teachers and children, the more we have come to realise that there are a number of underlying patterns that seem to be repeated endlessly in all sorts of variations and blends. Christopher Hampton categorises seven basic plots including tragedy. There seems to me to be a few basic patterns that are worth knowing about as simple stories can be built around these ideas.

1. Problem/resolution.
   This is the basic pattern – everything is all right, there is a problem and it gets sorted out.

2. Beating the monster.
   In some senses, this is the same pattern. Remember that monsters, ogres and dragons are all metaphors for anything bad in our lives. In this tale – everything is all right; a monster arrives and has to be overcome – often by the weakest person. The monster could be an ogre, a savage dog, bullies, a nasty teacher, disease or unemployment.

3. Warning.
   This is a very handy version of the above two plots. You begin with a warning such as 'do not play near the canal'. Of course, the main characters do whatever it is that they are not supposed to do – and get into trouble, need a rescue and have learned a lesson by the end.

4. Quest.
   This is another very common pattern. In it a character is given a task and has to make a journey to complete it. From 'Lord of the Rings' to 'Red Riding Hood', literature is full of journey stories.

5. Wishing/barriers.
   Many stories involve a character who really wants something but is stopped by a barrier – in the end the barrier is overcome and often the main character attains their heart's desire but it is often not worth having! Life is all about overcoming barriers from trolls who block the way to wicked emperors.

6. Lost/found/chased.
   In 'lost' stories either the character gets lost or loses something precious. In a 'finding' story the finding of something significant leads into the tale – from corn to magic brushes! In a chase, a character is pursued.

7. Cinderella.
   This is the most common pattern around the world. It is the tale of someone oppressed who through diligence, kindness or loyalty manages to win through – sometimes with the assistance of a 'helper'. I suppose the little red hen is a form of Cinderella – though she gets there on her own!

8. Magical powers.
   In these tales some form of magical power or trick is involved in the story.

9. Character flaw.
   Character flaw stories are about characters that through some flaw find themselves in trouble. Often by the end they have learned a lesson or changed.

10. Fables/myths/legends.
    These types have their own patterns – many of which can be imitated and innovated upon or borrowed to create new tales. Family stories (recounts from children's own lives), for instance, are especially helpful as they can be fictionalised as if they happened to someone else and turned into a story.

11. Family Stories.
    A rich resource for storymaking is our own experience. Start from retelling anecdotes and then fictionalise these by changing the names of characters and resetting the tale.

Tell it – draw it – retell it

When children are working independently, it can help if they get used to preparing their story in two ways:

1. Deciding what will happen – talking the ideas through and drawing a map, storyboard or mountain to capture their ideas.
2. Telling the story and retelling it – turning the decisions into story language.

The teacher has to model this – deciding, telling, drawing, retelling and so on.

Record or Write it

Now it may well be that you are just going to make a story up for the fun of it – and it will never be recorded in any way. However, there are various possibilities for recording inventions:

Making up stories

1. Children retell their story to another class;
2. Tape or record the story;
3. Video – use a digital blue camera;
4. Draw the story map and annotate;
5. Draw the main events onto a story board;
6. Map the main events onto a story mountain;
7. Draw or write notes on the main events into a flow chart – which provides a simple paragraph planner;
8. Write the story up as it develops onto a flip chart or blank big book.

A few thoughts on character

Characterisation is not easy for young children. In the main their characters move through the stories with events happening to them – rather than the characters causing events. One simple way to introduce the idea of characterisation is to provide a menu of 'feelings' to choose from. These might be positive or negative feeling, e.g.

Kind	Sad
Generous	Lonely
Happy	Angry
Brave	Spiteful
Clever	Greedy
Excited	Cruel

Incidentally, it can be fun to have lists of characters, settings or feelings or dilemmas in sets of six – and use a dice to select randomly. Anyway, as soon as you say '*Once upon a time there was a foolish fox who....*', the possibility of something interesting occurs. The fox is foolish so what silly thing might happen? Deciding on an emotion leads you into thinking about how a character's disposition will influence events – what the character might 'say or do'. Genuine characterisation is shown through action and dialogue.

Furthermore, if a character is lonely at the start of the story – by the end they may well have found a friend and be happy! In this way, simple character development can be achieved.

Character description should be kept to a minimum as it can interfere with the story. Try bringing a character on with a descriptive 'sentence of three', e.g. *He wore a red cloak, pointed shoes and a tall hat.*

Other tips on characterisation are:

■ Do not have too many characters – one or two will do;
■ Choose a good name for your characters;
■ Try re-using the same character in different stories so you get to know her/him well;

- Build up a bank of stock characters to call upon;
- Use a menu of 'feelings';
- Think about or act out what a character might say or do.

A few thoughts on dialogue

Dialogue is hard. It needs to be modelled many times – and practised many times. Begin by using a new line when someone speaks. Then move onto speech bubbles. Then pop the bubble and leave the speech marks.

Provide simple reminders on the wall and on story cards to show the children how to set out dialogue. Avoid stories that have lots of dialogue in them. Collect powerful speech verbs on the wall, story cards or in their writing journal – and make sure they use them! Introduce in year 2, the adverb – *he muttered <u>mysteriously.</u>*

When writing dialogue, ask the children to think about what this character might say (remind them about the character's 'feeling'). Add in a stage direction to show what the character is doing as they speak, e.g. *'Come here,' whispered Bill,* **<u>as he ducked under the car.</u>**

A few thoughts on settings

Use setting cards to provide a simple bank to call upon. Use the digital camera to take photos of local places that can be added to the bank of settings. To describe settings can be simple, if you show the setting through the character's eyes – what they saw:

Shamila looked at the dark forest. The trees were taller than a house and in between them strange shadows flickered!

Have a wall chart or page of 'settings' words to support the children when writing. The children only need one or two details to build the picture for the reader and then they can get on with the rest of the story.

A word about Story Mountains

Some schools have used the basic story mountain pattern as a structure from year 2 onwards. The mountain is displayed in each class with the connectives attached at the relevant places. Older pupils will of course begin varying the pattern. But at least it provides a simple frame for everyone's stories.

A word about 'and then'

Recently, a girl asked me how to avoid saying, 'and then' when telling or writing. This is quite simple. If you can feel that you are about to say 'and then', pause. Stop. End the sentence and omit the words 'and then'. Leave a slight space or pause. Then start the next sentence.

Chapter 4 Using the bank of stories

I have provided six stories for each year. I have also provided some ideas for innovations. In the appendices, I have shown one extra 'journey' story (with a warning) that would be good for any year group + a story map so that you can see what one looks like. Keep your maps simple and clear – with a pathway that shows the route through the story. Add in a few connectives or prompt words if need be and use colour to make hard bits memorable.

If you look carefully, you will see the various language features such as connectives or sentence variation built into the stories – try to emphasise these and provide an action as these are the aspects that you want the children to learn. The language bank and action bank are in the appendices.

If you find the way in which I have written the stories makes it hard for you to say them fluently and rhythmically then please do adapt and alter.

Good luck – and have fun! You are passing on an imaginative world and creating lasting metaphors in children's minds. These stories will become beacons in the dark night – in eighty years from now these tales will still be alive inside the children's minds. You are passing on something lasting and of the most infinite mystery to do with the human spirit and how we cherish it within ourselves and within the children we teach and learn with.

Pie Corbett 2007.

Nail Soup

Once upon a time there was a traveller who came to a village on the edge of the great forest. There he met an old hen wife. Unfortunately, the traveller had not eaten for days and his tummy was rumbling like thunder.

So, he opened his sack and took out a rusty pot. First, he made a roaring fire. Next, he put the rusty pot onto the fire. After that, he tipped in some water. Finally, he took out a shiny nail and dropped it in! Then with his trusty, rusty spoon he sipped the soup.

'So what does it taste like?' asked an old hen wife who had been watching curiously as he popped the nail into the pot.

'My, this soup tastes as good as the sky itself… but I've been using that nail all week and its grown a little thin so it needs a few vegetables,' said the traveller. So, the hen wife fetched one onion, two carrots and three potatoes. The traveller popped them into the pot.

After a while, the traveller took out his trusty, rusty spoon and sipped the soup.

'So what does it taste like?' asked an old hen wife who was still watching curiously.

'My, this soup tastes as good as the sky itself… but it needs a chicken rib or two,' said the traveller. So, the hen wife fetched some chicken ribs and the traveller popped them into the pot.

After a while, the traveller took out his trusty, rusty spoon and sipped the soup.

'So what does it taste like?' asked an old hen wife who was still watching curiously.

'My, this soup tastes as good as the sky itself… but it needs some herbs,' said the traveller. So the hen wife fetched some fresh herbs and the traveller popped them into the pot.

After a while, the traveller took out his trusty, rusty spoon and sipped the soup.

'So what does it taste like?' asked an old hen wife who was still watching curiously.

Then the traveller took out his trusty, rusty spoon and tasted the soup. 'Mmmmm, this soup is better than a slice of sky pie!' After that, he shared his soup with all the villagers.

Eventually, Old Goody Gardener said, 'How wonderful to have nail soup.' Everyone agreed. Wishing that she too could make such wonderful soup, Goody Gardener eyed the nail. So, the traveller polished the nail on his coat, gave it to her and set off for another village and, perhaps, another bowl of nail soup.... or stone soup.... or pebble soup!

Lazy Jack

Once upon a time there was a lazy boy called Jack who lived with his mother. Unfortunately, they were very poor. His mother worked hard spinning. However, Jack did nothing. In the summer, he basked in the sun. In the winter, he dozed by the fire.

One day his mother said that if he didn't work for his porridge, she would throw him out of the house.

So Jack went to work for a farmer. At the end of the day, he was paid one bright, new penny but on the way home he dropped it in a stream.

'You stupid boy,' said his mother, 'you should have put it in your pocket.'
'I'll do so next time,' promised Jack.

The next day, Jack went to work for the farmer again. At the end of the day, he was paid with a jar of milk. Remembering what his mother had told him, Jack tipped it into his pocket.

'You stupid boy,' said his mother, 'you should have carried it on your head.'
'I'll do so next time,' promised Jack.

The next day, Jack went to work for a miller. At the end of the day, he was paid with a tom cat for catching mice. Remembering what his mother had told him, Jack tied it onto his head.

'You stupid boy,' said his mother, 'you should have tied it up with string and lead it along behind you.'
'I'll do so next time,' promised Jack.

The next day, Jack went to work for a baker. At the end of the day, he was paid with a roast chicken. Remembering what his mother had told him, he tied it up with string and pulled it along behind him.

'You ninny hammer,' said his mother, 'you should have put it in your nap sack.'
'I'll do so next time,' promised Jack.

The next day, Jack went to work for a cattle-keeper. At the end of the day, he was paid with a donkey. Remembering what his mother had told him, he tried to squeeze it into his knapsack.

On his way home, Jack passed the home of a beautiful girl. Long ago, the doctors had said that she would not speak until she had laughed. Consequently, her father had promised that the first person to make her laugh could marry her.

Along came Jack with the donkey on his back and its legs poking into the air. Now the sight was so strange and so comical that the girl burst out laughing! So it happened that Jack became both married and wealthy, despite his foolish ways.

Snip snap snout –
My story is out!

Jack and the Beanstalk

Once, not twice, but once upon a time there lived a poor widow who had a son called Jack.

One day she told Jack to sell their cow, Milky-white, at the market. So Jack walked and he walked and he walked until he met a little old man.

'If you sell me your cow, I'll give you not one, not two not three, not four, but five magic beans,' said the old man.

But when Jack got back home, his mother was furious and she threw those beans right out of the window.

Early next morning, Jack woke up to find that the beans had grown higher than the sky. So, he climbed and he climbed and he climbed till at last he reached the sky. There he found a road and at the end of the road was a giant's castle.

Inside was the giant's wife, ugly as a troll's doll. 'Quick, hide in the oven. My husband is coming!' she whispered, opening the greasy oven door.

Sure enough, along came the giant with three bags of gold, thumping, thumping, thumping. 'What's that I smell?' he roared. 'Fee-fi-fo-fum, I smell the blood of an Englishman. Be he alive or be he dead, I'll use his bones to grind my bread!' Luckily, the giant fell asleep. Hoping the giant would not catch him, Jack grabbed the gold, climbed down the beanstalk and escaped. His mother was mightily pleased.

But in the end, the gold ran out so Jack climbed and he climbed and he climbed till at last he reached the giant's castle.

Inside was the giant's wife, ugly as a troll's doll. 'Quick, hide in the oven. My husband is coming!' she whispered, opening the greasy oven door.

Sure enough, along came the giant with his hen that laid golden eggs, thumping, thumping, thumping. 'What's that I smell?' he roared. 'Fee-fi-fo-fum, I smell the blood of an Englishman. Be he alive or be he dead, I'll use his bones to grind my bread!' Luckily, the giant fell asleep, snoring like thunder. Hoping the giant would not catch him, Jack grabbed the hen, climbed down the beanstalk and escaped. His mother was mightily pleased.

But in the end, Jack was not content so he climbed and he climbed and he climbed till at last he reached the giant's castle.

Inside was the giant's wife, ugly as a troll's doll. 'Quick, hide in the oven. My husband is coming!' she whispered, opening the greasy oven door.

Sure enough, along came the giant with his golden harp, thumping, thumping, thumping. 'What's that I smell?' he roared. 'Fee-fi-fo-fum, I smell the blood of an Englishman. Be he alive or be he dead, I'll use his bones to grind my bread!' Luckily, the giant fell asleep, snoring like thunder. Hoping the giant would not catch him, Jack grabbed the golden harp and began to run. But the harp called out, 'Master! Master!'

Jack climbed down and down and down but the ogre followed him. As soon as Jack reached the bottom, he called out. 'Mother, bring me an axe!' As soon as he had the axe in his hands, Jack chopped the beanstalk not once, not twice but three times. The ogre felt the stalk shake and quiver till he began to topple down, down, down to the earth… and the beanstalk came toppling after!

So the ogre broke his crown and Jack – why, he married a princess and they lived happily ever after. Or so they say!

Cric crac –
Put that story back
In the old man's sack!

Midas

This is the story of King Midas and this is the way that I tell it.

Early one morning, the gardeners in King Midas's palace found Silenus sleeping in the rose gardens. He was snoring as loud as a giant's rumbling belly. So they bound him hand and foot with bindweed and dragged him before the King.

At first, Midas was cross but Silenus enchanted him with wonderful stories. Enchanted, Midas listened to tales of magical journeys past frightening whirlpools to impossibly beautiful cities where the fruit of youth grew and silver spires reached high to the sky. Midas sat spellbound for five whole days.

In the end, Silenus returned to his home and the god Dionysus granted Midas one wish to reward his hospitality. At once, Midas said, 'Pray, grant that all I touch be turned into gold.'

At first, this seemed like a good idea. He turned stones to gold, then a table and chairs but when he sat down to eat – the food turned to gold. Then he tried to take a sip of water and that too turned to gold. The days rolled by and Midas was surrounded by gold but he grew thinner and thinner. Why, he dared not touch his own children just in case he turned them into statues. Standing in his palace, he saw gold as far as the eye could see but he also saw his own end!

Eventually, Midas pleaded with Dionysus to free him from the curse of his own greed. Laughing, Dionysus flung back his head and roared his disgust. He told Midas to bathe in the source of the River Pactolus. Even now, many thousands of moons later, the river still has specks of gold on its sandy banks.

Now you would have thought that Midas had learned not to fool around with the Gods but he went to a musical contest between Apollo and Marsyas. When Apollo won, Midas began to argue, shouting and yelling at the umpire who happened to be a River-God. His punishment soon appeared for he sprouted a pair of donkey's ears!

Midas felt so ashamed that he pulled on a cap and kept his bristly ears hidden from sight. But his hair grew and it grew till in the end he had to visit his barber. Midas threatened the man with death if he told anyone but the barber found it impossible to keep the shameful secret to himself.

So late one night, when no one was looking, the barber crept down to the river bank and dug a hole. When nobody was about he whispered into the hole, 'King Midas has donkey ears!' Then he filled the hole and went away feeling much better. Unfortunately, a reed sprouted from the hole and when the spiteful, wintry wind blew it whispered the secret to all those who passed by! So, once again Midas felt the sting of shame.

Why Bats Sleep in the Day

Have you ever watched the bats flitting through the darkness at dusk? Have you ever wondered why bats only come out at night? Well, once upon a time the sun shone all day like a golden coin and the moon shone all night like a silver discus. My, the moon was so bright that no one could ever get any sleep!

So, God gave Bat a wicker basket tied up so tight that whatever was inside could not escape. Bat wondered what he was carrying but dared not even peep. God told Bat to fly to the moon. So, he flew and he flew and he flew but the journey was long. In the end, poor bat had to stop and rest, hanging upside down with his wings folded like an old umbrella.

While bat slept, some of other creatures became curious and opened the basket. Out leapt darkness! One moment, it was quite bright and the next second it was darker than the heart of a mountain. It was darker than the inside of a stone. It was darker than the bottom of the ocean because God had trapped night in the wicker basket and now it was let loose.

Of course, everyone was grateful for the silvery light of the moon. And poor old bat still has to sleep all day because he is so busy at night frantically fluttering about trying to catch the darkness to take it to the moon. I'm afraid he'll never manage to capture so many shadows. Surely they will outwit him every time?

Why the sky is so high

In Nigeria, they tell the story of how once the earth and the sky were close together. Now this is the way that I tell it.

Once, the sky was so close that if you ever felt hungry, you could reach out and snap off a slice to eat. No one bothered growing any crops and many people were so lazy that they cut off more than they needed. They just threw the leftovers onto the rubbish heap.

The sky grew angry and warned the humans, 'If you take more than you need, I will move myself far away where you can no longer touch me.'

For a long while, everyone was respectful. But in the end, a greedy man cut off a chunk without thinking. It was too big for the man, too big for his wife, too big for the family and too big for the neighbours so they just threw the leftovers onto the rubbish tip. Yes, they just cast aside a slice of the blue sky!

At this, the sky grew angry and, in a moment, it deserted the earth and fled far away into the distance where it still waits today. From that time on man has had to toil in the soil, growing his own crops. The sky has warned man that there is enough for what we need but not enough to feed man's greed.

Now that is how they used to tell the story in Nigeria and the sky it thought that it was safe at such a distance, way out of man's greedy reach.

But man's greed knows no bounds and the story is not yet at an end. For even though the sky is many miles high, man has managed to make a few many more cracks where the sun pours through. The crops have begun to dry up, for the sun is punishing the earth! Will man stop this time or will the sky take more steps back till it is just a dot in the distance? Imagine a world without the beauty of blue and beware!

The Mystery of the Hare and the Moon

Have you ever gazed at the moon and wondered about the strange dark shapes on its white face? Let me tell you the story of how those shapes appeared on the moon.

In India, long ago, there were four friends – the hare, the otter, the elephant and the monkey. They loved each other dearly but most of all they loved the hare for the hare was so kind that all the animals thought she must truly have a heart of sunlight.

Hare told the animals how love lights even the darkest night, even the darkest heart. Hare told the animals about how the stars in the sky hold the future and the plants in the forest hold health. Hare told them how to care for each other and even the tiger, the wolf and the eagle sat and listened. Hare's love shone from within her like the great sun itself. All the animals felt warmer for sitting near her love.

One night, Hare had an idea. She had been walking near the village and had seen a beggar scrabbling for food at the village rubbish tip. 'Tomorrow is the day of rest. Let us all make a sacrifice and do some kind act to feed a human who is less fortunate.' The four friends all agreed.

The next day, otter caught a fish and left it at the edge of the village by the rubbish tip. Elephant picked bananas and left them near the roadside. Monkey gathered mangoes and left them where the beggars slept. But Hare could not find a gift to give. Hares just eat grass and that was of no use to any human! What could she do?

At that moment, Hare paused with a terrible thought. She had remembered that humans eat meat! It was too awful to think about but Hare knew then that she had to sacrifice herself if she was to keep her promise.

Now it just so happened that a God was watching and listening and decided to put Hare to the test. Would an animal really be prepared to sacrifice itself for a beggar?

Wandering down the path towards Hare, hobbled an old beggar, leaner than a bag of bones. 'Make a fire,' suggested the Hare. Moments later the scarlet flames were roaring and the Hare leapt into the dreadful fire – but the God snatched Hare from the flames, saying, 'such love must be made known to everyone.' So it was that Hare was placed on the moon where still to this very day you can see her shape every night as a reminder of her powerful love. She shines down on us all as we sleep and as we drift on the riverboat of dreams.

And they do say, that even if we forget the hare, she will always be watching over us. For she will never forget us, however slim our faith becomes, however slender our hope.

Little Red Riding Hood

Once upon a time there was a girl called Little Red Riding Hood because she always wore a scarlet coat with a crimson cap.

Early one morning, her mother said, 'Take this basket of food to your grandmother but whatever you do, don't dilly dally on the way.' Into the basket she put – a slice of fruit cake, a juicy apple and a large, yellow cheese.

So, Little Red Riding Hood walked and she walked and she walked till she came to the middle of the forest. The forest was dark and she could hardly see where she was going. Tired from so much walking, Red Riding Hood rested under a huge tree. Whistling happily, along came the woodcutter. 'Where are you going?' he asked and Little Red Riding Hood explained.

Unfortunately, a grey wolf was hiding behind a tree and listening to everything that they were saying. Greedily, it licked its thin lips, pawed the ground and ran off to find Grandma's cottage.

When Little Red Riding Hood reached Grandma's cottage she let herself in. Grandma was lying in bed but she looked very strange.

'Oh Grandmama, what great big ears you've got,' said Little Red Riding Hood.

'All the better for hearing you with,' replied Grandmama.

'And what big eyes you've got.'

'All the better for seeing you with,' replied Grandmama, leaning forwards.

'And what big hands you've got,'

'All the better for hugging you with,' replied Grandmama, smacking her lips.

'And what big teeth you've got,'

'All the better for ..... eating you with!' shrieked the wolf triumphantly, leaping from the bed.

Little Red Riding Hood screamed as the wolf opened its huge jaws.

Luckily, at that moment, the woodcutter dashed into the cottage and killed the wolf with not one, not two but three mighty blows from his axe! For he had seen the wolf following Little Red Riding Hood through the forest.

To the Edge of the World

Once there was a man who was so unlucky that he had lost his house, his job and even the shirt off his back! So he set out to find an answer to his problems.

He walked and he walked and he walked and soon he came to a rocky valley where there was a wolf, a lean wolf, a mean wolf with fierce red eyes and sharp white teeth.

'I'm trying to find an answer to why I am so unlucky and to see if there is anything that can be done about it,' said the man to the wolf.

'If you find someone who can help, will you ask a question for me?' growled the wolf.

'Of course,' replied the man.

'Very well, ask why I am so thin and what can be done about that?' So the man set off again and he walked and he walked and he walked until he came to a place where a huge oak tree was growing.

'I'm trying to find an answer to why I am so unlucky and to see if there is anything that can be done about it,' said the man to the tree.

'If you find someone who can help will you ask a question for me?' asked the tree in a voice made of rock.

'Of course,' replied the man.

'Very well, ask why my branches are dying and what can be done about that?' So the man set off again and he walked and he walked and he walked until he came to a place where a girl was crying bitterly.

'I'm trying to find an answer to why I am so unlucky and to see if there is anything that can be done about it,' said the man to the girl.

'If you find someone who can help will you ask a question for me?' sobbed the girl.

'Of course,' replied the man.

'Very well, ask why I am so sad and what can be done about that.' So the man set off again and he walked and he walked and he walked until he came to the very end of the earth. Clouds billowed, rain drifted and buzzards swooped across the valley.

There he met an old man with a long white beard.

'Why am I so unlucky and what can be done about it?' he asked the old man, peering at him with curiosity.

'There is plenty of luck just waiting for you,' chortled the old man, nodding his head.

So, sooner, rather than later, the unlucky man had answers to the other questions and he set off. Excited by the prospect of his good fortune, he ran and he ran and he ran. Soon he came to the place where the girl was crying.

'I've been promised some luck and I'm on my way to find it,' he shouted.

'I'm pleased for you,' sniffed the girl, 'but what about me? Why am I so sad?'

'That's easy – you are sad because you are lonely,' replied the unlucky man.

'What can be done about it?' sniffed the girl.

'That's easy – you must marry the first handsome young man who passes by and the pair of you will live happily ever after.'

'Will you marry me then?' asked the girl, staring at him intently.

'Sorry, I'm on my way to find my luck!' shouted the unlucky man. He ran and he ran and he ran. Soon he came to the place where the oak tree was waiting as patient as time itself.

'I've been promised some luck and I'm on my way to find it,' he shouted.

'I'm pleased for you,' grumbled the tree, 'but what about me? Why are my branches dying?'

'That's easy – they are dying because your roots are blocked by a treasure chest and can no longer suck up enough water,' replied the unlucky man.

'What can be done about it?' grumbled the tree, hopefully.

'That's easy – you must stop the first strong young man who passes by and ask him to dig up the treasure chest and take it away.'

'You look strong – will you dig up the chest and take it away?' the tree asked, staring at him intently.

'Sorry, I'm on my way to find my luck!' shouted the unlucky man. He ran and he ran and he ran. Soon he came the place where the wolf was waiting, looking leaner than ever, looking meaner than ever.

'I've been promised some luck and I'm on my way to find it,' he shouted.

'I'm pleased for you,' growled the wolf, 'but what about me? Why am I so thin?' Eyeing the man, the wolf pawed the ground.

'That's easy you are thin because you are hungry,' replied the unlucky man.

'What can be done about it,' growled the wolf, staring at him intently.

'That's easy – you must stop the first fool that passes by and eat him up.

And so he did.

Mulenga and the cherries

Tales like to travel. Now, this one came from Greentrees in Zambia. John heard it from Cynthia Chilufyah who wrote it down. He had taught her one of my stories and now I'm passing her story on to you. So, let's play 'pass the story' – pass this one on and we'll see how far it can travel....

One day Mulenga went shopping with his mother. Their first call was at the green grocers and while his mother was buying some fruits, Mulenga looked longingly at a box containing lovely red cherries.

'Help yourself to a handful, Mulenga,' said the green grocer, but Mulenga did not move.

'I'm sure you like cherries, don't you?' asked the puzzled shopkeeper, and Mulenga nodded his head quickly. Thinking that the boy was too shy to hep himself, the greengrocer went to the box and gave Mulenga a large handful.

When they left the shop, Mulenga's mother asked him why he had not taken the cherries when the greengrocer had told him to.

'Well you see, Mummy,' replied Mulenga, 'his hand is twice as big as mine!'

Matale comes to Supper

It was well known that Matale was greedy, selfish and never shared anything with the other villagers.

One day, his grandmother invited Matale to supper. 'Don't be late,' she said, 'and make sure that you wash your feet because I don't want any dirt dragged inside!'

That evening Matale dressed in his best clothes, rubbed a little coconut oil into his skin and washed his feet. When he reached his grandmother's, he found that she had burned all the grass around the hut.

'Go down to the river and wash those feet. You're covered in smuts from the grass,' said his grandmother. So off went Matale to wash his feet.

When he returned, he could smell the supper cooking but his grandmother still would not let him in. Pointing to his grubby feet, she muttered, 'I'm sorry, but you'll have to go back and clean them again.' So off went Matale as fast as he could with his belly rumbling.

When he returned, his grandmother still would not let him in. 'I'm sorry,' she said, 'you've taken so long that I've finished the food and beside, your feet are still dirty!' Wearily, Matale plodded home with an empty belly and much to think about.

Now that is the story of Matale 'What was that all about ?' asks old grandmother, smacking her teeth, cracking her knuckles and wearing her wisdom in a toothy grin!

The King of the Birds

Once upon a time there was a farmer called Yann who was so poor that in the winter the wind sneaked in through the cracks in the door and the snow fell down the chimney pot. Why he was so poor that his little old mother sat in her bed with an icicle hanging from her nose!

Early one frosty morning, Yann went out to feed his cattle at the barn. The snow lay in a thick crust on the fields, ice glittered on the path and the water trough was frozen like a mirror.

At that moment, Yann heard a strange noise. Something was caught in the brambles beside the barn. It was a beautiful, white horse. Calming the horse down, Yann pulled the brambles to one side and set the horse free.

To his amazement, the horse turned and spoke to him. "Yann, I am King of the wild horses. For setting me free, I can grant you one wish. Come back at midnight when the moon is high and tell me your heart's desire.' Then the horse shook its mane, turned and galloped away.

All afternoon, Yann paced up and down, wondering what he should wish for. In the end, his ancient father came in, almost bent double with the weight of his years. 'Father, father. If you had but one wish, what would it be?' asked Yann.

'I'd wish for my eyesight. For I have been blind these last ten years.' Of course, his father was right! If he could see, his father might help with sowing the seeds and reaping the harvest.

But then, Yann's mother came in. 'Mother, mother. If you had but one wish, what would it be?' asked Yann.

'I'd wish for gold. Why, we are so poor that we will either starve or freeze to death!' Of course, his mother was right too! There was never enough to eat and the pinch of winter was dreadful!

But then, Yann's wife came in. 'Wife, wife. If you had but one wish, what would it be?' asked Yann.

'I'd wish for a baby to bring joy into our lives. Who will care for us when we are old?' Of course, his wife was right too! But then, so was his mother …. and so was his father! Yann did not know what to wish for.

At midnight, Yann made his way down to the old barn. The moon was like a white coin in the night and the stars speckled the darkness. It was icy cold. Thundering across the fields came the white horse. 'What is your wish?' it called to Yann. At that moment, Yann had an idea. At first it was just a seed of an idea but soon the seed took root.

Standing still, beneath the grinning moon and the speckled stars, he called out, 'I wish for my father to see our baby in a cradle made of gold!'

'Good wish,' whinnied the horse, galloping away. Yann made his way back to the old cottage and, as he came up the path, he heard a sound that he had not heard before coming from the bedroom. It was the sound of a baby crying!

Hamelin

This is the story of The Pied Piper of Hamelin and this is the way that I tell it.

In the year 1284, in the town of Hamelin, there was a plague of rats. They had rats in the ditches, rats on the floor, rats in the houses and rats in their britches! There were so many rats that even the cats had left!

But that year, a stranger came to Hamelin, dressed in a long flowing coat of many colours. Some people said it was Joseph but soon he became known as Brightman. He said that he could get rid of the rats for the right sum of money. The elders of the town agreed to pay him if only he could rid them of the rats.

Brightman took out his pipe and began to play. To everyone's amazement, the rats streamed out of the houses and followed Brightman. Rats, rats, everywhere, chased after Brightman out of the town, across the hills, squealing and squeaking till they came to the River Weser. Brightman strode into the river and the rats followed him only to drown in one swirling mass!

That afternoon, Brightman returned to the town but the elders refused to pay him any money. The days ran by like rabbits and still the elders tried to pretend that the rats had not been that much of a problem.

A month later, Brightman returned to Hamelin. Dressed in a scarlet cloak, wearing a strange mask, for one last time, he demanded his money. And one last time, they refused. So he took out his pipe and played. But this time it was not rats that followed him, it was the children.

Children, children everywhere, chattering and chortling into the mountains. Chattering and chortling, they ran after the piper, following his tune. Chattering and chortling into the distant hills.

And they were never seen again.

The Legend of the Green Children

It was harvest time.

We were down by the wolf-pits
Playing hide and seek
when we first saw them.

Stumbling out of the cave,
Blinking at the daylight,
Babbling strange sounds.

They stood stock-still,
shock-still –
and so did we.

For they were green –
green as the leaves on the may-time tree,
green as the grass that sways at the wayside,
green as the newly minted, spring time corn.

So we took them home and offered them bread –
but all that they would eat were beans from the pod.

As the days ran by, the girl learned to speak
but the boy grew silent and refused to eat.

But the boy grew pale and he took to his bed
and seven months on they found him dead.

But the girl married Lenna and told us their tale –
they came from St Martin's,
a sun less land
where the bright country can be seen
far across the great river.

Brother and sister,
they had followed their flock
into a cavern
where they heard the sound of bells
That lead them into our bright world.

Now she's grown older and her skin is like ours
but once in a while she wiles away the hours
back in the past, lost in another world,
a world of her memories,
a world of green.

Now, I'll never forget that first time we saw them –
the shock of seeing
skin of green.

And all of this happened in the reign of King Stephen
a cart horse's ride from Bury St Edmunds

– so says I, Ralph of Coggeshall.

Why Compassion Bears Fruit.

This is a story told by the Alur who live in Africa beside Lake Albert.

Once there were two brothers who went hunting in the bush. First they set some snares to trap birds. The older brother trapped a fat pigeon, but his younger brother only caught a spider. Feeling sorry for the spider, he set it free.

The next day, they went out hunting to set more snares. Once again, the older brother trapped a fat fowl but his little brother only managed to snare a bolt of lightning. It fizzled and hissed, crackling with energy. So the younger brother set the lightning free.

The following morning, the King told them to cut some new grinding stones so they could grind the corn. They tried and they tried and they tried but only made their axes blunt. Finally, the younger brother called to the lightning to help. With a crackle, the lightning split the rock into many pieces forming several perfect grinding stones. The King was delighted.

That evening, the King told them to bring him a star from the night sky. They knew this was impossible but they tried and they tried and they tried. Finally, the younger brother called to the spider to help. With a hiss, the spider threw out a sticky web across the night sky and trapped a star, dragging it back to the earth like a glittering crystal. Astonished, the King rewarded the boys with cattle for their family.

All this was because the youngest brother had not killed what he could not eat and had spared the spider and the lightning.

Skillywidden

Have you ever wondered what it might be like to capture one of the little people? Everyone knows that the little people have crocks of gold hidden. Well, this is the story of Tricky Dicky, my near neighbour who lived in Trevidga in Cornwall, and this is what he found.

Early one morning Tricky Dicky was out walking when he found a tiny pixie sleeping on a bank of wild thyme, covered in blossom. He was small as a cat and dressed in a green coat with sky-blue breeches and diamond buckles on his shoes.

'What can I do for you?' asked Skillywidden.
'Tell me where your gold is hidden,' said Tricky Dicky.
'I've hidden it in a sack,' said the pixie.
'Where is the sack?' asked Tricky Dicky.
'I've hidden it in a jar,' said Skillywidden.
'Where is the jar?' asked Tricky Dicky.
'I've hidden it in a hole,' said the pixie.
'Where is the hole?' asked Tricky Dicky.
'I've hidden it under a tree,' said the pixie.
'Where is the tree?' asked Tricky Dicky.
'I've hidden it in Sharpham Woods!' said the pixie.

So, Tricky Dicky picked up the pixie, popped him into his coat and walked off towards the woods.

They hadn't gone far when Skillywidden said, 'Tricky Dicky, you should go home right now. Your cows are in the corn!'

'Just hold your tongue,' snapped Tricky Dicky, 'I'm not going to be tricked by a pixie.' So, on they walked.

They hadn't gone far when Skillywidden said, 'Tricky Dicky, you should go home right now. Your sheep have broken out!'

'Just hold your tongue,' snapped Tricky Dicky, 'I'm not going to be tricked by a pixie.' So, on they walked.

They hadn't gone far when Skillywidden said, 'Tricky Dicky, you should go home right now. Your geese have flown away!'

'Just hold your tongue,' snapped Tricky Dicky, 'I'm not going to be tricked by a pixie.' So, on they walked.

They hadn't gone far when Skillywidden said, 'Tricky Dicky, you should go home right now. The roof has blown right off your cottage!'

'Just hold your tongue,' snapped Tricky Dicky, 'I'm not going to be tricked by a pixie.' So, on they walked till they came to Sharpham Woods. There were hundreds of trees.

'Now then Skillywidden,' said Tricky Dickey, 'Under which of these trees is the gold hidden?'

The little pixie pointed to one of the trees and said, 'That one!'

So, Tricky Dicky began to dig in the ground under the tree but it was no good. The earth was too hard. 'I need a spade,' he said to the pixie, 'But if I go home now, I'll never remember which one of the trees has the gold hidden underneath.'

Then Tricky Dicky had a good idea. He took off his blue scarf and he tied it to the tree.

He was about to run home when Skillywidden piped up, 'Tricky Dicky, have you finished with me, kind sir?'

'Yes,' said Tricky Dicky as he dashed of home to fetch the spade.

Cheekily, the little pixie waved his hand and said, 'Then may you have all the luck that you deserve!' And at that moment the little pixie turned into a huge black crow and flew away over the hedges, calling, 'Here I am, Mammy!'

Now, when Tricky Dicky got home what did he see?

The cows were in the corn!

Worse than that, the sheep had broken out!

Worse than that, the geese had flown away!

And worse than that, the roof had blown right off his cottage!

But Tricky Dicky wasn't in the least put off. He could only think about the gold. Grabbing his spade, he ran straight back to Sharpham Woods.

Now, when he got to the woods what do you think that he saw?

A tree with a blue scarf tied round it.
And another tree – with a blue scarf tied round it.
And another and another and another – every single tree had a blue scarf wrapped round it.

Poor Tricky Dicky ran from tree to tree but it was no good.

'That pixie tricked me,' said Tricky Dicky, as he made his weary way back home.

And even till this day,
Tricky Dicky will say,
'Never ever trust a pixie!'

Beowulf

Now long ago in the land of the Dane there was a terrible monster. Grendel. Even its name was enough to terrify.

It was in the time of King Hrothgar when he built his great banqueting hall on the edge of the swamps. Every night, they feasted till late. But Grendel heard their celebrations from the depths of the swamp. He heard their laughter. He heard their joy. And he heard their drinking songs. He smelt the roasted ox and he felt hunger gnaw at his belly like a rat in a trap. So hungry that in the depths of the night, while the kings and his men slept, Grendel came stalking across the marshes and up to the great oak door.

He came three times in all and left nothing behind him but the taste of blood and fear. Reluctantly, the King abandoned the hall and left it deserted – except for the sparrows and the gathering dust.

But one day the great hero Beowulf arrived. His wooden ship carved through the whale roads and when he landed, Beowulf leapt from the bow into the waves. Clutching a handful of sand, he laughed. "I will slay this monster of yours," he boasted to the King.

So it was that the Danes returned to their hall. Once again the sound of singing and laughter rang through the oaken beams. They roasted an ox, they drank fine mead and great stories were told.

Eventually, they fell asleep. But Beowulf waited in the great hall with only his sword as his friend. Gradually, the shadows filled each corner. The sparrows settled in the rafters. Silence held its breath!

Slipping silently through the marshes, Grendel came. Like a dark plague staining the fields, Grendel dragged his terrible soul up to the hall and walked through the door as if it was not there. He tore one sleeping soldier in half and crunched on his bones. Then he reached out for Beowulf who waited, crouching in the shadows.

Beowulf seized Grendel's arm like a metal vice and clung on, digging deep into his flesh. Howling, Grendel swung this way and that, but it was no good. Beowulf's grip was tighter than steel. The soldiers woke and tried to fight the monster but could only see the vaguest of shapes. Their swords slipped through the shape and had no effect. Grendel could not escape Beowulf's grasp and with one last terrible wrench pulled away, his arm tearing from his shoulder.

Howling with pain, Grendel slouched back towards the swamps to bathe the bleeding stump. And to die. Meanwhile, Beowulf nailed his trophy to a beam where it stayed for many months, rotting away till in the end there was nothing left.

But that was not the end of the story. For what they did not know was that Grendel's mother had watched him die and now she wanted revenge...

You see, every age has its own monsters. As soon as one has been defeated, another rises to take its place.

But that is another story for another time.

Bedd Gelert

Do you have a pet? Well, this is the story of Prince Llewellyn who lived in Wales when the country was covered with forests. One day, the King of England gave Llewellyn a wolfhound called Gelert as a present. Gelert loved his master and was the kindest, most gentle of animals.

Now Llewellyn's wife had died and his only family was his baby son. Gelert loved the baby too and would spend hours with the baby tugging at his fur. But Gelert was gentle and never once growled.

One afternoon, Llewellyn set out hunting deer. He left Gelert with the baby knowing that he would protect him with his life.

Hours later, as the evening sun set, Llewellyn returned. To his surprise, Gelert limped towards him and collapsed at his feet, exhausted. Llewellyn knelt down and stroked his faithful dog. But he pulled his hand away for Gelert was covered in blood.

With a cry, Llewellyn rushed to his baby's room and there met a terrible sight. The baby's cradle was overturned; blood stained blankets lay on the floor and the baby was nowhere to be seen.

The Prince grabbed the dog, drew his sword and in his grief he killed Gelert. "Murderer!" he howled. "You have killed my only son." Poor Gelert stared up at his master and watched Llewelyn's familiar face as his life slipped away.

As Gelert's body stilled, Llewellyn heard a whimper from behind the cradle. Rushing to the spot, he flung the cradle to one side and there under a blanket was the baby – and beside him lay the great body of a dead wolf.

So it came to Llewellyn in one moment what had happened. Gelert had attacked and killed the wolf to protect the baby. With a howl of pain and regret, Llewellyn turned back to Gelert but his faithful friend lay quite dead.

Now even to this day you can see Gelert's grave near Colwyn Bay in the village of Bedd Gelert. There in a field where the sheep bleat in spring you will find the small stone that Llewellyn used to mark the memory of his greatest friend that by his own hand he slew. Killed in haste by grief.

Icarus

And so it was that Daedalus, the inventor, found himself dragged before the great King Minos, in the dead of night with the rush lights flickering.

'You!' roared the King, 'you are the one who built the labyrinth. You are the one who led to my Ariadne being taken away by Theseus. It is your fault!'

'But your majesty, you asked me to build the labyrinth...'

'No buts – take him and his snivelling son to the tower.'

And so it was that Icarus found himself dragged to the tower in the dead of night, up the winding steps and into the top room.

There the days ran by like rabbits. Every morning, the oak door opened and a bowl of food and a loaf of bread were shoved into the room. Once a week, a new candle was provided so that at night they were not in complete darkness. A glimmer of light from a glimmer of kindness.

Ranting and raving, Icarus paced up and down shouting about what he would say to the King. But Daedalus spent his time leaning on the windowsill staring out across the city towards the distant hills of Crete and the sea that lay like a thin blue ribbon in the distance.

Daedalus stared down the sheer sides of the tower to the people far below, who scurried about their daily business like so many ants.

One day he looked up at the great buzzards as they wheeled high in the sky, caught on the thermals, spiralling upwards and he saw a feather falling. Daedalus snatched the feather and as he held it in the palm of his hand he had an idea. At first, just a seed of an idea, but soon it took root.

Daedalus gathered the candle stubs and hoarded them, so that at night they had to sit in the darkness. He took the bread and crumbled it, scattering the crumbs on the windowsill. At first the sparrows came fluttering down. Later, the white finches and magpies came. Some days he used to lure down the buzzards with small pieces of meat. Whenever a bird landed, Daedalus would lean out and *'snitch'*, he would grab a feather.

When the pile of feathers was enough, he melted the wax in the midday sun and used it to bind together the feathers into two mighty pairs of wings. He tore his shirt into strips and made bindings so that he could tie on the wings.

Early one morning, as the sun rose and before the guards were awake, Daedalus strapped the wings onto Icarus and himself. Carefully, they stood on the edge of the window ledge, toes curled over the edge, holding hands.

'Whatever happens Icarus, keep gliding straight – don't let a thermal catch you and send you too high. The sun is too hot for our wings to last. At first we'll dip down so hold your arms firm and we shall glide across the sea towards Sardinia and safety.'

Without warning, he tugged Icarus and they swooped down. As the air filled their wings, they straightened up and began to glide over the city, across the hills and above the sea.

'I can fly, I can fly,' yelled Icarus with excitement. Tightening his grip on his son's hand, Daedalus flew straight ahead. But full of freedom, having escaped Minos, Icarus was in no mood for heeding his father's sense and he let go of his father's hand, swooping and dipping and diving – looping the loop till a thermal caught him and Icarus began to spiral upwards.

'Glide straight!' yelled Daedalus but already Icarus was too far from his father's calling, spiralling up and up. So high, so certain, so full of himself that he did not hear the steady drip, drip, drip nor did he notice the feathers falling. In one moment he hung in the air no longer circling upwards and then in the next moment he dropped like a rock. Plummeting down towards the sea, Icarus saw the blues and the greens and the white crests of the waves rushing up to greet him.

And Daedalus too saw his son fall, 'crack-smack'! Into the sea! Wretchedly, Daedalus glided on to Sardinia, with his heart heavier than Mount Olympus itself, knowing that his son had died by his own invention, by his own invention...

Now that is the end of the story of Daedalus, the inventor, and Icarus who flew too high, too high, too high...

Crying Wolf

Every day Pieter took the sheep out onto the mountainside and every day he grew bored.

Now his father had told him that if he saw a wolf he should cry out, 'Wolf, wolf!' and all the villagers would come running to rescue the sheep.

So one day when Pieter was very bored, he hid behind a rock and called, 'Wolf, wolf!' He giggled to himself as the villagers ran huffing and puffing up the hillside. But they were furious when they found that it was just a trick.

Day after day, Pieter carried out his trick until in the end the villagers didn't bother to come running.

Unfortunately, one day a wolf did come out of the forest. Pieter called and he called and he called but the villagers just shook their heads and muttered, 'Oh that's just Pieter calling wolf again.'

At the end of that day, Pieter went back home with no sheep left but he had learned a terrible lesson: *Liars will not be believed even when they tell the truth.*

The Mouse and the Lion

Late one night Mouse was out and about hunting.

Unfortunately he wasn't looking where he was going and sooner rather than later he bumped into Lion.

Luckily, Lion had just eaten and was not hungry. 'Please don't eat me,' pleaded Mouse. So, Lion let him go.

Unfortunately, later that night, some hunters trapped Lion in a net.

Luckily, Mouse was passing by. Sooner rather than later, Mouse began to nibble at the ropes to set Lion free.

While the hunters slept, Lion and Mouse ran off into the forest both free and friends *– for the strong may be weak and the weak may be strong but kindness is a strength that all may own.*

The Old Man and the Donkey

An old man and his son were taking their donkey to market to sell. The donkey walked ahead of them and they both walked behind, talking of little bits of this and little bits of that.

Sooner rather than later, an onlooker said, 'What's this? You've got a donkey and yet you make this poor little boy walk in the heat of the day?' Thoughtfully, the old man put the little boy onto the donkey's back and off they set. The boy enjoyed resting his legs.

Sooner rather than later, another onlooker said, 'What's this? You lazy little boy making your old grandpa walk while you ride at your ease!' Embarrassed, the little boy clambered down and the old man struggled onto the donkey's back himself. The old man enjoyed resting his weary limbs.

Sooner rather than later, another onlooker said, 'What is this? You let such a young boy run along beside you, while you rest on your donkey's back!' Gratefully, the boy climbed onto the donkey's back as well.

So on they trotted.

Sooner rather than later, a final onlooker said, 'What's this? You let a poor old donkey carry both of you. Surely, it cannot be your donkey. You are treating it so cruelly!' So that poor old man no longer knew what to do for the best.

Confused, he bound the donkey's legs together with some cord. In that way, they tried to carry the donkey strung out on a pole between them all the way to the market.

Everyone laughed at such a ridiculous sight! It upset the old man so much that he set the donkey loose in the fields and went back home with his grandson, empty-handed.

And the moral of the story is that if you try to please everyone, you will end up pleasing no one – not even yourself.

The Canal

Early in the morning, Tom and I made our way down to the canal. My Mum had told us not to play there, but Tom said that it was safe. While we were walking across the fields, we chatted about last night's football game. Moodily, Tom kicked at the molehills. Cheltenham had lost again!

After ten minutes, we reached the lane, crossed over and ran down to the canal. Carefully, we peered in. It was thick with green weed. The water was still and black. Only the odd bubble broke the surface. It looked deep. Excitedly, Tom grabbed my arm and tugged me over to the old oak tree. Where the branches stretched out across the canal, an old rope dangled down.

Although it looked dangerous, Tom grinned at me. He took a run up and leaped out over the canal. After he grabbed the rope, he swung backwards and forwards whooping like a siren. Although I was laughing, inside my heart was thudding. I knew that I would have to swing over the canal next. Tom jumped off. Happily, he handed me the rope.

For a moment, I hesitated. "Are you scared?" asked Tom, looking at me. I did not want him to think that I was a coward. Warily, I ran back and leapt out. I sailed across the canal, skimming the water with my heels. As I reached the other side, I let go and crashed down onto the bank. Tom laughed and leapt out for the rope.

He meant to swing across and join me but half way over the rope snapped. Tom crashed down into the water. At first, I laughed but then I remembered. Tom couldn't swim. Desperately, I leapt in. At first, I could see nothing – just darkness and weed tangling my feet. But then I saw red! It was Tom's hoodie. Frantically, I grabbed and tugged him to the side.

Twenty minutes later, we were standing in Mrs Jenkins' kitchen. I had to explain what had happened and Mrs Jenkins gave us both an earful. Then I had to go back to my house where my Mother gave me a force eighter. After all, she had warned me often enough. The canal was dangerous. We'd been lucky.

The Party

It was the first birthday party that Gary had ever been to and he was feeling a little bit nervous, but also excited. He arrived at exactly eight o'clock and soon realised that most of the children were from his class. First they all sat down to eat tea. James had a large cake in the shape of a football. Everyone sang 'Happy Birthday' and Gary ate twelve sausage rolls and drank three cups of cola. His Mother didn't let him drink coke at home. She reckoned that it gave you bad teeth!

When they had finished eating, Mrs Jenkins took them all into the sitting room and everyone had to play games. They began with 'musical chairs' and then to quieten them down they played 'pass the parcel'. After that, she brought out a large bag. They all took it in turn to put their hand into the bag to see if they could guess what was inside. Mrs Jenkins called it a 'feely bag'. To make it more exciting, she turned the lights down.

Now Gary didn't like the idea of sticking his hand into a bag. He had seen a film about Flash Gordon who had had to stick his hand into a tree trunk which had a scorpion inside it.... and the memory still made him shudder. Gary waited quietly, hoping that if he kept still and said nothing them maybe Mrs Jenkins wouldn't notice him. But it didn't work. 'Now then young man, pop your hand in and have good feel around.' Gary's hand seemed to have a life of its own. He didn't want to put it into the bag. But in it went! At first, he felt nothing. Then he touched something round like a marble but it was slippery. Gary knew what it was. It was an eyeball!

Gary's scream was so loud that his Mum reckoned that she heard it from three roads away. Within a second, everyone else was screaming too and Mrs Jenkins flung the bag into the air. It took quite a while to settle everyone down after that – but, in the end, she opened the bag and showed Gary what he had touched. It wasn't an eyeball. It was a peeled grape! Everyone laughed and Gary felt a little bit foolish.

Later on, Gary's Mum came to fetch him home. 'Say thank you for having me,' she reminded Gary, as they left. It was dark outside. Gary held his Mum's hand all the way home. As they walked down the street, she dug her hand into her coat pocket and brought out a small bag. 'Here, have a toffee, love,' she said. Gary stared at the bag. Inside he could hear the sweet papers rustling. Gary loved toffees – but for the first time in his life, he said,' No.'

The Talking Skull

A tale from West Africa.

A hunter was out in the bush looking for food when he tripped over a white skull that lay under a tree. Stooping down to pick it up, he muttered, 'How did you get here?'

To his amazement, the skull replied, 'Talking brought me here.'
As you can imagine the hunter could hardly believe his ears. But the skull carried on, 'Just over the next hill, you will find plenty of berries – but don't tell anyone.'

The hunter put the skull down, ran over the hill and picked as many berries as he could carry.

When he got back to the village, he could not help telling everyone that not only had he met a talking skull but also it had been able to tell him where to find food!

Soon the King got to hear about the hunter and the talking skull. He told the man that he must either be a liar, a madman or a fool.

Of course, the hunter protested his innocence. He took the King and his guards out into the bush to the place where the skull lay under the tree.

'Watch this,' said the hunter as he stooped down and picked up the skull. Gently, he whispered, 'How did you get here?' but the skull was silent. So the hunter tried again and again but still the skull said nothing. Again and again he tried but to no avail.

'I was right,' said the King. 'You are a liar, a madman and a fool all rolled into one.' He ordered the guards to kill the hunter for trying to deceive him.

When they left, the sun beat down on the bush. After a while, the white skull turned to the hunter's head, and it said, 'How did you get here?'

And so it was at last that, with understanding, the hunter's head replied, 'Talking brought me here!'

The Photo Album

Curious, Dominic peered at the faded photograph album. 'But who is it?' asked Emily, pointing at the shadowy figure standing beside Grandpa. The photo had been taken on their last summer holidays. They could remember everyone else – except for the man beside Grandpa.

Grandpa lived on the other side of town and one bus ride and half an hour later, they were sitting in his kitchen. He fussed over a pot of tea and set too boiling eggs and making Marmite soldiers. Once tea was served, Grandpa put on his old wire-rimmed glasses and began to thumb through the album.

'That one,' said Dominic, as Grandpa stared at the photograph. There was a long pause as Grandpa adjusted his glasses and squinted, leaning close up to the page. Then he held it away from himself, taking another look. He shook his head and made a tutting noise. 'So, who is it?' asked Emily, impatiently tapping her foot.

There was a long silence and Grandpa shook his head again. He looked up at them and Dominic could see that grandpa's eyes were watery and looked sad. 'That is my brother,' he replied as he closed the album and set it down on the table. 'But we don't remember seeing him that day' replied Dominic, watching Grandpa as he settled back in his favourite chair.

'I'm not surprised you don't,' whispered Grandpa, settling himself back into his favourite armchair. 'Because that is my brother Johnny alright.' There was a long pause and then he added, 'and he died in the Second World War!'

Dominic could feel the hairs on the back of his neck bristle! How could it be possible for someone so long dead to appear in a photograph? But Grandpa was talking and explaining. 'You see, we made a pact. If anything happened to one of us, then the other would try and come back. Make contact. I'd forgotten that till just now when I saw him in the photo.'

Grandpa shook his head in disbelief and chuckled to himself. Picking up the album, he thumbed through looking for the photo. But when he found the right page, there was no sign of his brother any more. Just the shadow of a tree, falling like a dark stain beside where Grandpa stood.

That happened twenty-five years ago. I still have the photo. Some days, if you look at it in the right light, you can still see the vague shape of another person, trapped in a shadow, frozen in time, but smiling, smiling out of the past.

Kidnapped!

Somebody was coming up the stairs! We ducked down behind an old crate and waited. I could feel my heart thumping like crazy and my throat felt tight and dry with the dust.... and with fear. What if we were caught? The strange girl glanced at me in the semi-gloom and grinned. I thought she was trying to be reassuring.

The door opened and we could hear someone coming in. There was a pause and then a torch flickered on. Its beam pierced the darkness, seeking us out, nosing into all the dark corners. I held my breath and tried to make myself as small as possible. After a few moments, the light switched off. Whoever it was stood quite still. We could hear breathing. Then the door shut and the footsteps went back down the stairs. I let out a sigh of relief.

As we clambered out of the window and slithered down the wet roof, I was trying to remember how I had got into such a mess.

It had only been half an hour ago, when Mum had sent me down to the chippie with a tenner and strict orders for no vinegar on her chips. When I reached the McDonald's roundabout, I couldn't help looking at the old house. It was ready for demolition, which was a shame because we had used the windows as target practice! It was then that I'd seen it. A light at the window. Then a face, mouthing something. I stood there staring. It was a girl mouthing a word. And the word was HELP.

That's how it happened. I'd found a way in round the back through a broken window. Half a minute later and I'd found her, trapped prisoner in an upstairs room. She'd only just finished telling me that she was the American ambassador's daughter Cindy Breakwell and about the ransom money, when they had returned to move her to a safe house.

So there we were, balancing on the wall as if we were walking the plank. Five minutes later and we were back at Mum's. 'So, where's the fish and chips?' she asked, eyeing Cindy suspiciously.

Half an hour later, Cindy's Dad arrived in an embassy car. That was the talk of St Petroc's estate for weeks. That night it wasn't just fish and chips. He took us all out for a big meal and the next day there I was. In the papers. A hero.

The Cobbler of Krakow and Smok the Dragon of Wawel

In the days when trees could cry and cats could fly there lived in Poland, underneath Wawel Hill, beside the Vistula River, a terrible dragon called Smok Wawelski.

First, Smok stole their cats and dogs. Next, he ate their sheep and cows. In the end, Smok paid his attention to grabbing young maidens!

Soon it was the turn of the King's daughter to be fed to the dragon. In desperation, he offered his daughter's hand in marriage to anyone who could rid the city of this terrible beast.

Princes came and Princes went. Some ran as soon as they clapped sight on Smok. Others ventured under the city and were never seen again. In the end, a cobbler called Krak came to the city.

'You'll never defeat the dragon,' said the King, noticing that the cobbler had no sword.

'Do not worry,' replied Krak, 'I will give him a meal that he will not forget in a hurry!'

First, Krak took a leathery cow's skin. Next, he stuffed it full of the hottest herbs and spices with a bag full of sulphur! After that, he sewed the skin together to make it look like a dead cow.

Finally, Krak threw the mighty meal down into Smok's lair calling, 'Dinner time, my beauty!'

The dragon ate it up in one gulp. First, he felt a burning pain. Then his stomach roared like fire. Finally, the dragon flew to the River Vistula where he drank and he drank and he drank till the river was almost dry. The more he drank, the more his stomach swelled. It swelled and it swelled and it swelled till in the end it burst with a huge bang.

So it was that the cobbler married the princess and became King Krak. Why he was so popular – that they named the city after him – Krakow.

Mombe and Momo

Everyone in the village had been married. Everyone – except for Mombe and Momo. Momo was so gentle that he never stood up for himself but Mombe had such a bad temper that nobody ever dared talk to him.

One day Momo went hunting in the forest. He took his bow and arrows and padded through the jungle as quiet as a trapdoor spider threading a web. In the end, he shot a pair of plump pigeons.

Triumphant, Momo made his way home through the twilight, as the evening grew colder. Far above the stars began to speckle in the night sky. But on the way he met Matale, the great rock python. He would make a good skin, thought Momo, plucking an arrow. But the Matale pleaded, 'Have mercy on me for I am cold. Take me to bathe in the warm river.'

Sorry for the python, Momo carried the great snake, like a huge necklace threaded round his neck, down to the river. Matale slipped into the river and slithered under the warm water. 'Thank you gentle friend,' said Matale lifting his great head out of the water, 'I have felt your loneliness. Throw the pigeons into the river and then take whatever the water spirits send you.'

Momo obeyed and as soon as the pigeons hit water, it grew red and opened up like a huge scarlet mouth.

Momo stretched into the mouth and pulled out a red gourd. When he reached home he cut open the gourd and out stepped a beautiful girl who was as kind and gentle as you could wish. She fetched water from the river, scrubbed his clothes and tended the hens daily. Soon everyone knew Momo and his beautiful wife.

Mombe wanted such a wife too, so he asked Momo what had happened. As soon as Momo had told him the tale, Mombe set out to catch himself a pair of pigeons.

On his way back in the cool of the evening, Mombe came upon Matale, shivering in the bush. Mombe drew an arrow and was about to kill and skin the python when Matale spoke up, 'Have mercy on me for I am cold. Take me to bathe in the warm river.'

But, Mombe snapped, 'Make your own way!' So, Matale slithered through the bush till he came to the river's edge. Slipping into the river, Matale slid under the warm water. 'I have felt your loneliness. Throw the pigeons into the river and then take whatever the water spirits send you,' hissed the python.

Mombe obeyed and as soon as the pigeons hit water, it grew red and opened up like a huge scarlet mouth.

Mombe stretched into the mouth and pulled out a knobbly pumpkin. When he reached home, he cut open the pumpkin and out stepped the ugliest girl that you ever saw. She boxed his ears, kicked his pants and tugged Mombe by the nose. Poor Matale was bossed, bullied and beaten. He had to fetch the water, sweep the floor, tend the hens, hunt in the forest, and collect the honey from the wild bees. Why she worked him from dawn till dusk!

Mombe blamed Matale and the river spirit. But everyone else knew that he only had himself to blame.

The Blue Fish

Once there was a girl whose mother died. The villagers buried her body in the rich, red earth beside the river. After that, the girl woke every day at dawn and drove the long-horned cattle down to the river and onto the hillside. In the evening she drove them back again.

One day, her father decided to marry again. But from the first moment that the woman entered their life, she hated the girl. She hated her so much that she fed her no food. Day by day, the girl grew thinner. She grew so thin that her arms looked like chickens legs, her ribs stuck out and her eyes lost their shine. She began to look like death itself.

When she drove the cattle onto the hillside, she searched for berries and roots to eat. Some days she might find a bird's egg to crack into her mouth. At night, she lay, took to the shadows, in the corner of the hut, and lay with her legs tucked up tight for that way the hunger felt less.

One morning, as the cattle drank from the river the girl knelt down at the river's edge. She was thinking of her mother and crying. As her tears hit the water a great shape appeared, rising up from the depths. It was a fish, a huge, blue fish.

To her amazement, the fish opened its mouth and spoke. 'Climb into my mouth.' The girl stepped into the fish's mouth and it began to swim down through the cool water till it reached the bottom. There it spat her out.

And she was in another place where there was a bush growing and underneath the bush, in the shade was a cloth. On the cloth was enough food for a family. So she ate the cheese, the bread, and sweet yams until her tummy was tight. Then she stepped back into the fish's mouth. It swam up, up through the cool water towards the burning heat above. As it swam, she could hear it singing, 'Oh child be brave, when I am dead, bury my bones in your mother's grave.'

Now she did not know what the words meant but she would never forget them.

That night, she did not have to curl up tight. She lay down, full and content. So it was day after day, the fish took her down and fed her. Soon her eyes began to shine, her face filled out and she regained her strength.

Now late one evening, as the sun dipped over the shoulder of the distant mountains, the girl returned to the hut, dry and dusty. But the mother was waiting in the doorway of the hut. She grabbed the girl and said, 'Who is feeding you?' the girl she said nothing but shut her mouth tight as a clam. 'Who is feeding you?' but the girl she said nothing. She just curled up on the ground. Then the woman took a burning brand from the fire and beat the girl on her bare back, hissing, 'Who is feeding you?'

In the end, the pain almost swallowed the girl whole, so she whimpered, 'The blue fish, down by the river.' The woman threw the brand back into the fire and settled down to wait for her husband's return, while the girl crawled into the shadows and curled up. Her back stung with the pain.

When the father returned, the woman began to moan, 'I've been poisoned!' she cried, clutching her belly. 'Only blue fish will help – there's one down by the river.'

So the husband took a burning brand from the fire in one hand and a spear in the other. He ran across the dark plain till he came to the river. Waiting by the pool, he stared at the surface of the water. At first, there was nothing – only the slightest ruffle as the wind blew. But then a great dark shape rose up out of the depths. The blue fish broke the surface, opened its mouth as if to speak but – thwack! The spear tore into the fish's flesh. Grabbing the fish, he began to run back to the village. By the time he reached the hut, the fish was quite still. Grasping the fish, she disappeared into the hut.

Early the next morning, the girl woke up, slipped out of the hut and drove the cattle down to the river. She ran straight to the great pool and stared longingly into the water – but the glass was empty. That evening she came down from the hillside and waited but the pool was stiller than stone.

When she got back to the hut, the woman stood in the doorway, holding a bowl. 'Here,' she said, 'I've made you soup. Fish soup. Blue fish soup.' The girl staggered back and could not even touch the bowl.

She lay in the shadows, in the corner of the hut, feeling her misery as sharp as the raw wounds on her back. But the woman put a stool in the middle of the hut and began to eat from the soup bowl till, in the end, she had licked it quite clean.

When dawn broke, the girl woke. She could see the woman slumped on the stool with the soup bowl spilled onto the floor. Then she noticed hundreds of white specs – tiny flecks of bone. Fish bones. At that moment, she recalled the fish's song, 'Oh child be brave, when I am dead, bury my bones in your mother's grave.' At last, she knew what the song meant.

Gathering every last scrap of bone, she tiptoed out of the hut and drove the cattle down to the river. There in the rich red earth beside the river, she buried the fish's bones next to her mother's grave. Her heart was as heavy as rock itself.

That evening, as the sun streaked the sky scarlet, she made her way back to the grave and to her amazement a bush had grown there. Already, the leaves were deep green and shiny. It had one beautiful white flower, tinged with blue. She pressed the flower against her cheek and felt its cool touch and smelt the sweet scent. Then she noticed, tucked beneath the bush was a cloth and on the cloth was bread, cheese and a juicy yam.

So it was every day. She drove the cattle down to the river, went to the bush and there would be another flower and more food. Till one day the king's soldiers found the bush. They were laughing and joking. One of them tried to pick a flower for his girlfriend but it was impossible.

Now they went back and told the King about the amazing white flowers that could not be picked. That evening the girl was by the bush. On it were some bread and cheese but also a pair of leather sandals. She began to tie one on, strapping the leather thong round her leg. As she did so, she was thinking about how she could run barefoot anywhere now without getting thorns in her soles. But at that moment, she saw the King approach for he was curious about the flowers and had come to see for himself.

The girl took fright and began to run, one sandal on and one sandal off till soon she was just dust in the distance. The King was left standing, holding one sandal in his hand, staring into the distance for the girl.

'In one month's time, we will call all the girls here and see whom the sandal fits,' he declared.

So it was that a month later, all the local villagers came to see what would happen. One by one, the girls tried the sandal but it fitted no one. As evening drew on, the King ordered bonfires to be lit. Finally, they had tried everyone. 'Who is not here?' called the King.

Then it was that someone remembered the lonely girl who drove the cattle. She had come home late and was asleep in the hut.

So a runner was sent to fetch the girl – tired and unsure whether she was awake or still dreaming. She ran down from the village, towards the river, to where the fires flared in the darkness.

And there, right there, beneath the great dark canopy of night, freckled with stars, shaped by the silver moon, curved as a rhino's horn, the girl arrived. She went straight up to the King, took the sandal from his hand and began to strap it on. The crowd stilled to silence as the girl stood up. She walked to the bush, plucked a flower, pressed its cool petals to her cheek, and handed it to the King.

So it was that three days later, she became his wife. Oh there was such a feast. I wish you had been there. There was singing and dancing and storytelling – just there by the river, underneath the dark night with the stars speckling the great black back of heaven with the curved moon riding high.

And that is the end of the story of the Blue Fish.

The contest

The North Wind
had always been a bully –
heartless and only faithful
to the arctic snow.

Till one day,
the kindly old Sun
heard the north wind boast
that she was the strongest
of God's elements
– earth, wind and fire.

So to test, who was the best,
the Sun challenged the North Wind
to a contest.

'See that farmer
digging turnips –
the quickest to have his coat off
will be the winner,'
challenged the Sun.

So the North Wind blew
its iciest blast, stolen straight from Greenland's wastes;
a breeze that shrilled with icebergs and crystals....

But the farmer only shivered,
and tugged his coat closer.

So, the North Wind blew harder –
but the shriller the wind,
and the colder the blast,
the tighter the farmer tugged his coat.

Then the sun took over
and turned up the heat.

The farmer loosened his coat,
mopped his brow,
rested on his spade,
and in the end –
unbuttoned that coat
and flung it down.

So the North Wind fled
in a huff and a puff
and to this day
she is the coldest enemy
to the kindly Sun's glow.

Appendices

Resources

Poetry Anthology

* The Works Key Stage 2, edited Pie Corbett, Macmillan Children's Books – a large collection of poems suitable for reading, performing and as models for writing.

A few useful sources for more stories

- Barefoot Books – beautiful traditional tales collections worth buying – in particular, 'The Odyssey' retold by Hugh Lupton and Daniel Morden. You can buy both the book and an audio CD. This fabulous retelling brings the tale alive in a way that I have never heard before. It would make a feast for a year 5 or 6 class. – an absolute must have.
- Grimm's Fairy Tales – published by Routledge.
- Tales from Around the World by Jane Yolen – published by Pantheon
- The Magic Lands retold by Kevin Crossley-Holland – Orion.
- English Fairy Tales, retold by Joseph Jacobs – Puffin Books.
- Voyage – a series of guided readers – selected by Pie Corbett and Chris Buckton – published by Oxford University Press – one anthology per year across KS2. Short stories for reading and writing.
- The Bumper Book of Storytelling into Writing at Key Stage 1 by Pie Corbett – Clown Publishing. Practical resource book to help Key Stage 1 teachers.

Books and resources to help you develop storymaking

- Traditional Storytelling in the Primary Classroom – a very handy and practical book – by Teresa Grainger – Scholastic.
- Writing workshops: Teaching Narrative Writing at Key Stage 2 – by Pie Corbett – published by David Fulton. This focuses more upon crafting the writing and would make a useful adjunct.
- The Story Making Framework – the original planning framework and account of the research carried out by the International Learning and Research Centre is available by writing to: ILRC, North St, Oldland Common, South Gloucestershire BS30 8TL
- The Storymaker's Chest – a treasure trove of story cards, objects, posters etc. Ideal support for telling and writing. Published by Philip and Tacey.
- The Story Generator Cube – quickfire games using storymaking cards. Great for inventing new stories. Published by Philip and Tacey.
- Story Mats – 3 mats that are graded in difficulty – providing easy to use prompts not only for making up stories but also reminders about varying sentences, etc. Published by Philip and Tacey.
- Juggling Spelling and Juggling Sentences – great games for developing spelling and sentence construction skills. Published by Philip and Tacey.

Appendices

Web sites

two excellent sites for teachers – do check them.

www.storyarts.org/lessonplans/lessonideas/index.html
Lesson ideas and other activities such as treasure hunts.

www.sfs.org.uk
The website of the Society for Storytelling – worth joining. Also – good resources from Hugh Lupton – CDs and tapes that make a fantastic bank of tales for the classroom. Many links on from here into a whole new world of storytelling resources.

Action bank

Key connective	Suggested action
Once upon a time	open hands like a book.
Early one morning	hands to one side of head and pretend to wake up.
Who	finger circle index finger in air.
First	one finger up.
Next	2 fingers pointed to one side.
But	fingers down.
Because	hands out open palmed.
At that moment	
Suddenly	hands expressively open as if in surprise.
To his amazement	
Unfortunately	
Luckily	hands raised open as if thanking.
After/after that	roll hands over in turning gesture.
So	roll hands forwards and open as if giving.
Finally	palm facing audience like a policeman stopping traffic.
In the end	bring hands together as if closing book.
Eventually	

Fiction – reminder sheet

1. Vary sentences to create effects:
- Short, simple sentences – for drama and clarity: *Tom ran.*
- Compound sentences for flow: *Tom ran and Kitty walked.*
- Complex sentences to add in extra layers of information: *As Tom ran, Kitty ate the cake.*
- Questions to draw in the reader: *What was that?*
- Exclamations for impact: *Run for it!*
- Sentence of three for description: *He wore a dark cloak, shiny shoes and red trousers. The troll was tall, bony and very hairy.*
- Sentence of three for action: *Tom ran down the lane, jumped over the hedge and collapsed.*

2. Vary sentence openings:
- Adverb opener (how): *Slowly, ...*
- Connective opener (when): *Last thing at night, ...*
- Prepositional opener (where): *On the other side of the road ...*
- Adjective opener: *Tall trees towered over the river.*
- Simile opener: *As quick as a flash ... Like an eel ...*
- One word opener: *Sad, ...*
- 'ing' opener: *Running for home, Tim tripped ...*
- 'ed' opener: *Exhausted by the run, Tim fell over.*

3. Drop in clauses:
- Who: *Tim, who was tired, ran home.*
- Which: *The cat, which looked mean, ran home.*
- That: *The car, that was made of metal, melted!*
- 'ing': *Tim, hoping for silence, crept into the staffroom.*
- 'ed': *Tim, frightened by class 4, ate another cream bun.*

4. The 'ing' clause:
- Before: *Laughing at the dog, Tim fell backwards.*
- During: *Tim, laughing at the dog, fell backwards.*
- After: *Tim fell backwards, laughing at the dog.*
- Stage direction for speech: *"Hi," muttered Tom, waving to Bill.*

Practise – sentences types that relate to the text type and that will help progress.

Provide spellings and sentence types on cards and mats, etc. and in display.

List the key words and sentence features needed to make progress in your plans.

Fiction language bank

Reception Story Making Language Bank

Model language in everyday class activities using emphasis and actions.

Introduce

Once upon a time
Early one morning
And
Then
Next
Until/till
But
So
Finally

... happily ever after
... who ...

'Run' (he walked and he walked ...)

Description – a lean cat, a mean cat ...

Alliteration

Adverbs: Luckily/unfortunately

Prepositions: down, into, over, out, onto.

Year 1 Story Making Language Bank

Model language in everyday class activities using emphasis and actions

Consolidate	Introduce
Once upon a time	After/after that
Early one morning	One day
And	At that moment
Then	Soon/ as soon as
Next	Because
Until/till	Suddenly
But	By the next morning
So	To his amazement
Finally	In the end
	First
	If......
	Now
... who ...	... that ...
	... or ...
	... so that ...
	... when ...
	... where ...
■ 'Run' (he walked and he walked ...)	Repetition for effect
■ Description – a lean cat ...	Adjectives to describe
■ Alliteration	Simile – using 'as'
■ Adverbs: Luckily/unfortunately	Adverbs: Suddenly, immediately
■ Prepositions: down, into, over, out, onto	Prepositions: Inside, towards
■ ... happily ever after	

Year 2 Story Making Language Bank

Model language in everyday class activities using emphasis and actions

Consolidate		Introduce
Once upon a time	Next	Although
Early one morning	If	However
To his amazement	Then	
Suddenly	Now	
One day	Until/till	
After/after that	Soon/ as soon as	
And	But	
So	In the end	
First	Because	
By the next morning	Finally	
At that moment		
... who ...		... to ...
... when ...		
... that ...		
... where ...		
... or ...		
... happily ever after		
... so that ...		

- 'Run' (he walked and he walked ...)
- Description – a lean cat ...
- Alliteration
- Simile – using 'as'
- Adjectives to describe
- Adverbs: luckily/unfortunately, suddenly, immediately
- Prepositions: down, into, over, out, onto, inside, towards

Repetition for effect
Adjectives to describe
Adverbs: eventually
Prepositions
Simile using 'like'

Year 3/4 Story Making Language Bank

Model language in everyday class activities using emphasis and actions

Consolidate		Introduce
Once upon a time	Immediately	Later
One day	Although	When
Early one morning	However	Whenever
First	If...	Without warning
Next	So	Eventually
After/a while	Soon/as soon as	
Before	Then	
And	... until/till	
As	While/meanwhile	
But	In the end	
At that moment	Finally	
Suddenly		

... who ...
... while ...
... when ...
... that ...
... to ...
... or ...

- 'Run' (he walked and he walked ...)
- Description, e.g. a lean, grey cat
- 'How' starter, e.g. Slowly, ...
- 'Where' starter, e.g. At the end of the lane ...
- Alliteration and similes

- 'ing' clause starter, e.g. Running along, Tim tripped over.
- Drop in – 'ing' clause, e.g. Tim, running along, tripped over.
- Drop in 'who' clause, e.g. Tim, who was late, tripped over.
- Short sentences, questions, exclamations
- Sentence of three for description, e.g. He wore a red cloak, shiny shoes and a tall hat.
- "" plus speech verb/adverb

Year 5/6 Story Making Language Bank

Model language in everyday class activities using emphasis and actions

Consolidate		Introduce
Once upon a time	Although	Elaborate, e.g. Early one frosty
One day	However	morning
Early one morning	Later	
First	If …	
Next	So	
After/a while	As/soon/as soon as	
Before	Then	
But	… until/till	
At that moment	While/meanwhile/	
Suddenly	When/whenever	
Immediately	Eventually/Finally/	
Without warning	In the end	

… who …	… that …
… while …	… to …
… when …	… or …

- 'Run' (he walked and he walked …)
- Description, e.g. a lean, grey cat
- 'How' starter, e.g. Slowly,
- 'Where' starter, e.g. At the end of the lane …
- 'ing' clause starter, e.g. Running along, Tim tripped over.
- Drop in – 'ing' clause, e.g. Tim, running along, tripped over.
- Drop in 'who' clause, e.g. Tim, who was late, tripped over.
- Short sentences, questions, exclamations
- "" plus speech verb/adverb
- Alliteration and similes

- 'ed' clause starter, e.g. Exhausted, Tom ran home.
- Drop in 'ed' clause, e.g. Tim, exhausted by so much effort, ran home.
- Sentence of three for action, e.g. Tim ran home, sat down and drank his tea.
- Speech plus stage direction 'ing' clause, "Stop," he whispered, picking up his tea.
- Personification

Acknowledgements

Year 3

Nail Soup – I knew this as a child as 'The Soup Stone'. In the Russian version an axe is used.

Lazy Jack – I can remember my father telling me this story. There is a version in Joseph Jacobs 'English Fairy Tales', 1890. Also, collected by L.O. Halliwell in Yorkshire and published in 'Popular Rhymes and Nursery Tales of England' in 1849. There are some 200 versions also found in Asia, Africa and America!

Jack and the Beanstalk – This is the common version that I was told as a child. There is a version in Joseph Jacobs 'English Fairy Tales', 1890 – based on a version told to him by his nursemaid in 1860.

Midas – For details on this Greek myth, I referred to Ovid's (43 BC) 'Metamorphoses'.

Why Bats Sleep in the Day – There are many similar versions of this story that tell how night came. For instance, the White Mountain Apache have a story about how Badger carried night in a basket and Coyote, being curious, let it loose.

Why the Sky is so High – This is a story from Nigeria that a child in Hackney told me many years ago.

The Mystery and the Hare and the Moon – This is generally attributed to being based on a story about the Buddha who in an early incarnation offered himself as a sacrifice to Sakka, the chief God, who then painted a picture of Hare on the moon's face as a reminder.

Year 4

Little Red Riding Hood – This version is based on the one I knew as a child. It was collected by the Bothers Grimm around the end of the 18th century.

To the End of the World – This popular story is attributed to the english folk tale tradition by the French storyteller Abbi Patrix, though I am certain that its origins are Chinese or Japanese.

Mulenga and the Cherries – This story was passed onto me by John Camm who was teaching at Green Trees Primary School in Wiltshire at the time. He collected it from Cynthia Chilufyah – a pupil at Chiandra Basic School in Lusaka, Zambia.

Mutale comes to Supper – I've known this story for a long time but cannot remember where it came from. Let me know if you do, so that I can correctly attribute its source.

The King of the Birds – The story of 'three wishes in one' is well-known. There are all sorts of variants found around the world – spread rapidly by storytellers!

Acknowledgements

The Pied Piper of Hamelin – Joseph Jacobs has a version of this tale. Many believe that it was based on the Children's Crusade in the Middle Ages when children left their villages by their own will.

The Legend of the Green Children – certainly of medieval origin.

Year 5

Why Compassion Bears Fruit – A version of this tale was told to me by a group of children from Frogwell Primary School, in Chppenham. It is a story told by the Alur who live in Africa beside Lake Albert. There is a version in 'Essential African Mythology', by Ngangar Mbitu and Ranchor Prime. 'African Folktales' retold by Roger D. Abrahams is also essential as a reference for African tales.

Skillywidden – I was told a version of this story by a child in Cornwall. William Bottrell collected a version from Jack Tregar, 'an aged tinner of Lelant' around 1870, according to Neil Philip in 'The Penguin Book of English Folktales'.

Gelert – This rather grim tale is from Wales. You can actually visit the dog's grave – which I seem to remember is in the middle of a field!

Icarus – My parents told me this story – and I heard the storyteller Chris Smith tell a version. Robert Graves suggests that they may have escaped in a boat when Icarus fell overboard. The original is found in Ovid's 'Metamorphoses'.

Crying Wolf – This is supposed to be one of Aesop's fables.

The Mouse and the Lion – also attributed to Aesop.

The Old Man and the Donkey – This story was passed onto me by John Camm who was teaching at Green Trees Primary School in Wiltshire at the time. He collected it from Mutale – a pupil at Chiandra Basic School in Lusaka, Zambia.

Year 6

The Canal – This is my own story and based on a canal near my home where my children used to play.

The Party – This actually happened to me – many years ago. The memory still gives me a shudder!

The Talking Skull – a well-known African story. This version is based on one told by the Nupe of Nigeria. In some versions, the skull ends up saying, 'I told you to keep quiet!' It is worth remembering that in oral cultures stories and talk are held in high esteem. They say that 'when a man dies, a library goes up in flames.'

Acknowledgements

The Photo Album – My grandfather claimed that he met many ghosts though they always appeared just like ordinary people.

Kidnapped – The roundabout is in Aberdeen where I thought of this simple Enid Blyton type adventure.

The Cobbler of Krakow – perhaps the best known Polish story.

Mombe and Momo – This is an African Tale from Central Africa. A version was told to me by a group of boys in Frogwell Primary School in Chippenham.

The Blue Fish – a Cinderella variant from South Africa.

The Contest – a version of this story is found in Aesop's fables.